The
Deeper Magic

The Deeper Magic

By Matt Ford

To my children, Ethan, Caleb and Summer.

May you reach higher and go further.

We will stay

The Deeper Magic
Copyright © 2020 by Matt Ford

First paperback edition August 2020

Book design by Rachael Laing-Smith
Proof-read by Ben Leney
Forward by Dr Mollie Brown

ISBN	978-1-8381414-0-0	(paperback)
ISBN	978-1-8381414-1-7	(e-book)
ISBN	978-1-8381414-2-4	(audible)

www.wewillstay.co.uk

This is a powerful and convincing read, full of hard-won lessons learnt over thirty (forty?) odd years of pursuing God. I have read many testimony books, but this stands out as a practical guide to show parents and children how to disciple each other in the faith. It stems from the conviction that to get in on God's kingdom action, we need to be actively going for it. How do we do that? Matt Ford takes us through some ordinary and some far from ordinary experiences, distilling helpful biblical and practical principles, authenticated and amplified by members of his family reflecting on each chapter. I didn't want it to end. It is like taking a good long drink of a refreshing beverage. If this is the deeper magic, I want more of it in my life!

If you want to be stirred up to pursue Him more, read this book. If you long to see God's power for your family, what you read in this book will thrill your spirit and get you so expectant - picture your own children telling these stories in a few years' time. What we can dream and imagine, we can pray. And what we can pray faithfully, God will do in His time and in more wild and incredible ways than we can predict. Thank you Matt for being faithful to prophetic words on your life and writing this all down!

Ben Leney, MA : Pastor & Teacher, The Kings Gate Church, Bognor Regis

Matt and Kathryn are the real deal! Together with their whole family they live out the powerful message you will find here. Everything taught throughout the pages of this book has been born out of the furnace of both sacrifice and adventure. Deeper Magic is a call to jump with reckless abandon into the depths of the heart of a God who calls us into an extraordinary life. Read and be inspired!

Joe Gisbey, CEO Links International and Assistant Pastor Arun CC

If you have children, the way you raise them may be the most important thing you ever do. If you want your children to lead safe and conventional lives which fit in with the values of this world, you'd best avoid this book. But if you want them to become radical and joyful followers of Jesus, this book will be a great help.

I've known Matt and Kathryn for many years. What they've written is no more than the truth, and the lives of their children bear witness to this. They believe what Jesus says and live accordingly. In worldly terms they pay a high price for their obedience, but in the real, eternal kingdom they are rich; rich in joy, rich in wisdom and rich in what they have invested in the lives of others. Their family reflects this richness. This book is an insight into how families can be an asset to the kingdom of God.

Andrew Price, Co-founder The Coming Home Project & oversight HCC

Matt faces up to the reality of the challenges of being a Christian and especially a parent in the 21st Century. The heart of the book is to encourage the readers to put into practice their faith.

Throughout the book Matt shares experiences of how they operate to give each child a genuine experience of the Holy Spirit being at the heart of their family.

The strength of this book is that the Ford family that is written about is the Ford family that I have known for the last eight years. It is an honest testimony of a family seeking to follow God's way.

Phil Baker, Retired leader HCC & CAP oversight lead

Having known Matt, Kathryn and the children for many years, I have been so aware of the courageous path they have walked as a family. Mission and community, prayer and worship, hospitality and generosity are all deeply embedded in their decision to "seek first the Kingdom." So, how do we take hold of and lead a life that allows us to Dream Big with the tension of laying everything down? I believe Matt delivers a comprehensive and revelatory account of what this really means. It is almost as good as sitting at his table and catching up over coffee! Each chapter takes you on a new God adventure and draws you deeper to examine your own heart and motives. This is a book you won't want to put down!

Amanda Hills, BA : disciple-maker, stay-at-home mum of 4 & prayer warrior

With great humour, disarming punch and heartfelt pace, sharing both vulnerably and powerfully from his own 'being family and making disciples' experience ~ the Ford family's journey will challenge, provoke and challenge again to go deeper with your own family.

They are extraordinarily humble role models who lead by example in pushing through, pressing in, stepping out and embracing the Bible's truth for FAMILY in the 21st century. A raw, upbeat and brave narrative revealing a rare jewel of a family following hard after God: an absorbing, engaging and exciting read!

Cathie Jones, MA : Missionary & ambassador for Iris Global University & Director of International Relations.

Contents

Acknowledgements

As I look back over my God-life I recognise two things. That God has led me through despite my mistakes, doubts and stupidity and that people have cheered me on. Hebrews speaks of a 'cloud of witnesses' who have gone before us but I want to take a little moment to celebrate and thank those who have lined the roads of my journey and been there for me. Without you I, and we as a family, would not be where we are today and I would have probably given up or messed up or both. So, in some sort of quick fire chronology, here go my thankyous.

Thanks to my mum and dad for giving me a foundation of love and belief in Jesus and not throwing me out of the house when I was an idiot. To my brother who has become such a great man, fab leader and the person I have had the most laughs with. Thank you to Bridgwater Community Church for letting loose a young, immature Holy Spirit filled disciple. Thank you to YWAM Muizenberg for the adventures, fun and crazy Holy Spirit times in the Railway Station! Kings Bible School you showed me the rock which is Christ - a foundation that has withstood every storm. Thank you to Immanuel Church Winchester for giving me the chance to lead and for being a springboard to ministry and mission. Thank you to C.net and Tony Morton for believing in me and allowing me to be involved at such a deep level. To Kings Church Barking, amazing friends that I still miss today, for amazing encounters with God in the Manse and letting me go even when you didn't want to. To all who were part of Substance for the Soul - just wow! You showed me what was possible and we did it wearing boiler suits, breaking boxes and just having so much fun. To Arun Community Church for being a place to hide, a place to dream and a place to fly. For Iris Global for showing me in reality what I had only read about in history. People who literally run at hell with a bucket of never ending Jesus water. For Highworth Community Church, my friends and where we are living and believing for something great in our day.

To my children. For putting up with me, my occasional despair, the crazy ideas and for becoming my friends and my 'church' at home. To my wife who has never, in the 25 years I have known her, struggled in her relationship with Jesus, loves me so well and is my best friend. For all her help in completing this book and being on the journey that is this book.

To those who have read, fed back and have made up some nice stuff about me in the endorsements - love you. And to my brother-in-law Ben whose heart for God and English expertise has helped turn my writing into a real book.

And finally Jesus. It has always been you. I wish I was better for you but I love you with all my (little) strength, heart and soul. You are worth it all.

Matt Ford

Foreword

I have had the pleasure of journeying with the Ford Family for 9 years. We met in Mozambique and I was instantly drawn to them; they carried the heart of the father and walked in such surrender to God. They would pay any price for more of Him. I remember being utterly amazed at the way their children worshipped and hungered after God even at such a young age. There is something incredibly beautiful about seeing children worshipping with their whole heart before the Lord. Since then we have met across 3 continents and I have watched them and their children preach, prophesy, minister healing and love to many people with such confidence and genuine faith in God.

When I was a missionary in Cambodia they came to live with us for a short season and as a family they ministered to my broken heart and gave me renewed hope. I watched them consistently give themselves and pay a high price to walk in obedience and surrender to our King! This family carry a fire which they take with them all over the world! I have seen their young children minister to the prisoners, the poor and the broken with such confidence because they know who they are and whose they are. I had never met a family who were so united in their pursuit of the kingdom of God and so truly walked as disciples of Jesus.

This book is a goldmine of wisdom from parents who have managed to capture and sustain revival in their family. I believe this book, among other things, will inspire, empower and change the way Christian parents raise up their children as powerful lovers of Jesus. I have had lifechanging moments sat in their living room and encountered something which is sadly so often rare amongst believers. So often the children are excluded from our times of ministry and worship and we wonder why so many lose their desire for God as they grow older. This book has changed my life and it's one I believe every Christian should read; it's one that is so rich, profound and timely. With incredible vulnerability and clarity Matt pours his very heart out into the pages and so generously shares the challenges and victories of living in a lifestyle of radical obedience to Jesus. As you read this book you are invited into the lives of an extraordinary family; you will hear about their remarkable journey of pursuing God no matter what the cost! You will laugh and you will cry and you will never be the same.

This is not just for those with a family, it is a rallying cry for all of those who desire to walk the in the deeper ways of Jesus. Matt eloquently navigates us through some of the most foundational keys of the Christian walk; bringing the Bible to life and sharing powerful revelations he has received along the way. This book ignites hunger for greater intimacy with God and helps us to navigate some of challenges and tensions we face in today's Christian culture.

We are on the brink of a worldwide revival the likes of which has never seen before. This book is a gift from the Lord to help equip both parents and leaders in what it looks like to bring discipleship into every part of our lives, removing the secular/spiritual divide. As a parent and leader I long to see this happen in my own world but I so often don't know how; this book is full of great tools on how we can do this in a practical way seeing our children and those around us raised up as revivalists!

Mollie Brown, Medical Doctor, Iris Global missionary and BSSM graduate.

Introduction

'though the Witch knew the Deep Magic, there is a magic deeper still which she did not know. Her knowledge goes back only to the dawn of time. But if she could have looked a little further back...she would have read...a different incantation. She would have known that when a willing victim who had committed no treachery was killed in a traitor's stead, the Table would crack and Death itself would start working backward...'

Aslan: The Lion the Witch and the Wardrobe

On a hillside overlooking the sprawling panorama of the lake called Galilee, the God-man Jesus Christ tore back the curtains on life and how we were created to live it. The 'deeper magic'- those hidden treasures of God's Kingdom - flowed from his lips like a mighty torrent, washing away a relationship with God that had been based on outward manifestation and sweeping it instead deep into the arena of the heart.

'You have heard it said.........but I tell you.'

What was perceived as acceptable or important is brushed aside and something far deeper and more profound replaces it. How to really relate to each other, to God and to the world, is radically presented and suddenly the meek, poor and persecuted are centre stage.

To this day the message and the life Jesus lived flows, provoking, overwhelming and liberating every heart that is open to its touch.

It has touched our lives. It has changed everything.

So what's this 'magic' thing all about?

If you were to come and sit in my bedroom I could describe to you what lies beyond the closed curtains. I could tell you about the street outside, the bungalow with the wrap round garden or the cottage on the right. I could tell of the fading yellow salt bin on the corner or the grey BMW across the way. I could describe the neat rows of garden fences running left to right as the hill descends, or as we look further out, the green brown fields that then stretch in every direction. I could tell you how on a clear day the spired church at Lechlade, some miles north, glistens in the sunlight or about the distant smudge of the rolling Cotswold hills that frame the horizon.

It would be far better to just open the curtains.

Amidst the heat, dark red earth and smiley faces of northern Mozambique, our curtains were opened. Everything we had known before felt like a well described view and then suddenly the curtains were thrown back, and we could see. It became our defining moment - a threshold over which our whole life flowed to and away from. Transformed.

What we saw and continue to see is recorded here. It has changed our family and changed our ministry. What we saw was God's family. Family has always been the call. When Jesus taught his followers to pray, the revelation was to pray to Father, to Dad. Maybe more than ever there is a desperate need for great parenting and great leadership. Maybe more than ever these are maligned, twisted, confused and misunderstood.

This mysterious and challenging pilgrimage we call Christianity is an invitation into the heart of God. A God, as Samuel experienced, who does not look at the outward appearance but at the heart (1 Samuel 16:7). A God who wants to change the world by changing you. In writing a book about the most important thing we can ever do on the planet - to parent - both literal and spiritual children - this is a book first and foremost about your heart. Being and doing were never separated by Christ. He always divides to get to the root, the heart, for it is the wellspring of life from which all that you will do, for good or ill, will flow (Hebrews 4:12 and Proverbs 4:23).

The deeper magic is nothing clever or secret. It's all there in the Bible; it's just sometimes we don't really see it or know what it looks like today. So, this is an appeal to go below the surface, beyond the organising and the busyness to the things that have challenged our thinking, shaped our practice and radically altered our priorities.

The following chapters share what we have seen and the values we have gleaned. Each one of these has grown with time so this book shares our experiences but not chronologically. I wanted this book to be rooted in experience not just good ideas, which is why I try and share, openly and honestly, stories from our lives. To reinforce this, and so you know this isn't just my perspective, there is a family reflection at the end of each chapter. These are written by either my wife, Kathryn, or one of the children. This will hopefully give you a window into their experiences too!

If you are looking for a programme, strategy, or formula for how to be a good parent and bring up children, or for a course that produces mature disciples or a better leadership structure you will be disappointed. But if you wonder what it really can look like to follow Jesus in our day and our time, if you are hungry to see your family and those you influence and lead transformed, freed and in love with Jesus, then I offer you this. Our story. Just as the deeper magic changed Narnia and brought life, I pray that these simple treasures, discovered often through pain, failure and bucket loads of grace, change you and everything you do.

One

Control

'But whatever were gains to me I now consider loss for the sake of Christ. What is more, I consider everything a loss because of the surpassing worth of knowing Christ Jesus my Lord.'

Philippians 3:7-8

Like a trained sprinter I stepped into my blocks (well sat on a plastic chair), with the weight of my history behind me I took in the stadium (baking sun, dry red soil and a concrete floor), and stared down my race track (which strangely was an older gent with a beard and a glint in his eye).

This was my faith Olympics.

Rolland Baker started to speak, and I felt like I was on the cusp of destiny. My whole existence felt like it had drawn me to this point, here in Pemba, Mozambique, on the back of the craziest year of my life.

I had started that year, 2011, crushed. For over two years I had been working towards a teacher training post at a local primary school whilst juggling my work, studies and responsibilities. I had worked hard, put in hours at the school, developed new skills, seen doors 'miraculously' open and had jumped through every hoop that had appeared in my way. Alongside this I was still working for the Ambulance service, finishing my degree with the Open University, trying to be a good dad to my three children (Ethan, Caleb and Summer) and a great husband to my wife Kathryn... oh and that Christianity thing as well!

Becoming a teacher had always seemed a logical fit as both my parents trained and had worked as teachers, and it promised both better work-life balance and better career development than my current employment. It was our future. So the letter on the table telling me there were no spaces for me at the university, which would accredit my training, was devastating. The hope of becoming a teacher was in ruins and I felt like the children of Israel facing the Red Sea with the armies of Egypt behind them, just with less sand. I had nowhere to go and was out of options.

'What am I supposed to do now God?!' I shouted upward. I probably held my fist in the air and shook it to really underscore the point. A few expletives followed but even that didn't bring any answer. I felt angry. I felt a failure. I felt lost.

A couple of weeks later I was flicking through a copy of Christianity magazine at my parents' house and came across a job advert for a pastor in a church in Middlesbrough. It's funny how your life can hinge on a cold, seemingly innocuous, thought. 'So, there are churches who want to pay someone more than I currently earn, to do the thing I know I am called to do.'

No thunderbolt, booming voice, glory cloud, angelic appearance or even a pertinent Bible verse. Just a thought.

Graham Cooke says, 'If your current thinking has led you to a place you don't want to be, have another thought!' Perhaps that's the start of the real transformation that Paul calls us to in Romans chapter 12? Perhaps this renewing of the mind and discovery of God's will just begins with a thought, a different thought?

Eight years before this, in 2003, I had intentionally stepped out of church leadership, which paradoxically was the only thing I have ever wanted to do with my life. In a 24/7 prayer room at some unearthly hour of the night, despite bleary eyes and too strong coffee, God clearly said 'Lay it all down.'

There are times when God speaks direction and it's a nudge or a hint. This one was a clear call that I totally understood, even though I did not expect it. Jesus' words sprung into my mind from John chapter 12:24:

'Unless a grain of wheat falls to the ground and dies it remains only a single seed. But if it dies it produces many seeds.'

I had known instantly it was a call into a wilderness season. Into a season where I had to let go of my job working for a church and let all my hopes and dreams die. Where I had to let go of all my prophetic words and visions whilst leaving physically and spiritually where I was. The wilderness, a place of testing, silence and simplicity awaited. I knew that only He could bring me out and there were no shortcuts. A couple of weeks after this I received a prophecy during a ministry time at a leaders' conference that confirmed this call. 'Be strong. Let go. This next season is about your heart. God is after your heart. Trust Him.'

So, you can appreciate how I was then (in 2011) more than a little cautious, eight years, two more children, a mortgage and a nice set of golf clubs later. It wasn't about the job in Middlesbrough but the thought. A thought that grew into a question. 'Jesus is this the time? Do I take up my calling to serve the Church full-time?'

Being under authority is always a blessing, so I visited Becca, our church leader, to lay this at her feet and trust for wisdom. We were part of Arun Community Church, a thriving worship and community-centred local church in Littlehampton where we lived by the sea on England's south coast. Honouring does not mean obeying, it is something far bigger and more vital. Honour trusts God and respects and values the person. Honour enables us to let go of agenda and find faith with another. This is a beautiful truth that I will visit later in chapter 11.

I shared with Becca my recent discouragements and the question with which I was now wrestling. I knew it meant leaving Arun Community Church and moving away, so I was a little tentative. She, as ever, was brilliant. 'Go for it and I believe this is God.'

We went straight from that meeting to another one, like good church people!

Rodney Kingstone, who is now a very good friend, had set up a Prophetic School within our church and that night we would hear about what they had been doing and what the vision would be going forward. Unbeknown to any of us there, the new shiny prophetic team had been praying for us all the last few weeks and they began to share with different people what they felt God wanted to say. A lady called Pat, who I didn't know at the time, took the microphone and said the simplest and most profound thing anyone has ever given me from God. In her words:

'I was vacuuming, and God said 'Matt Ford.' I switched off the hoover and said 'What Lord?' and He said 'Tell him:

'Now my child. The time is now! Don't worry, he'll know what it means.'

Green light! Go, go, go! Tears streamed down my cheeks and I exchanged gobsmacked looks with Becca. Okay. That answers that one! So, we stepped out.

By May 2011, the future looked to be opening up like a kid's present on Christmas morning. Not currently connected to a church network I had gone back to my church roots and contacted a great leader I worked under years ago as part of the church stream C.net. I asked Billy Kennedy, who by that time was heading up the Pioneer network of Churches, if there was any opening for a full-time church leader. He was someone I had known for many years, someone I trusted and honestly my only real connection into other churches via relationship rather than through an advert (although I have nothing against adverts!). At the same time a church in a small market town called Highworth had contacted him, asking if there was anyone he could recommend for a full-time leadership post. Easiest day's work for Billy ever!

By mid-May we had visited Highworth Community Church a couple of times and felt good about it. Strangely enough they seemed to like us too. We were in the river, flowing where God led us, trusting the direction and speed and things were going well. September looked like a good natural time to aim to move by, so we put the house on the market and despite the forlorn face of the estate agent (this was the midst of recession) we had ten viewings in 14 days and three offers. Sorted. Next up Kathryn's job. We hadn't realised that, as a teacher in an Academy, she was required to give an entire academic term's notice for her job which meant we should have put the request in weeks ago. But we were flowing, we were in the river of His plans. So, free of panic or fear, Kathryn spoke to her head teacher who allowed a short notice resignation. Perfect.

Everything seemed to be coming together like a Michelin Star dish. The future was bright with anticipation and expectation high as we approached the summer. 'Here we go!'..... and then, well..... 'no we don't!'

A couple of the leaders from Highworth visited us in Littlehampton and very gently, kindly, shared with us that Highworth wasn't ready and might never be. Oh!

Suddenly, the river wasn't so much fun. Suddenly, we were careering towards a September deadline of no house, no future and one of us unemployed. Had we got it wrong? Did God say 'No' and we heard 'Go'?

That summer was a crazy mix of raging torrents full of fears and anxieties, mingled with deep pools of absolute trust and dependence. I think that's called faith. It all came to head as I sat on a mountain side on the remote Scottish isle of Rhona looking north towards the Hebrides. It was a holiday we had booked the year before so had to take despite having no idea what we were doing. I looked out across the North Atlantic and a thought dropped in. There was no emotion to it and yet it seemed to settle in the very deepest part of my being. Something so simple and yet so profound that it stands out as one of my pinnacle faith moments. 'If God really loves me then I have nothing to worry about.' And with that, without reserve, I chose to be all in and hold the hand of God, wherever He would lead me.

About a week before, I had been perusing the Iris Global website. Iris is a radical missions organisation pioneered by Heidi and Rolland Baker. Our only connection to them was that we had read their book that year and cried a lot. Their incredible, Bible like story, of a God of miracles and unboundaried love had shaken us to the core. We'd had this half an idea that perhaps all our readiness was so that we could go somewhere. Somewhere to grow our faith and soak in God's presence. But the standout feature had to be that it offered us all something - that it would be about us as a family all encountering God.

Our individualistic society has rubbed off on us, to the extent where we easily interpret our calling or God's purpose for our life as something that is for me alone. But your life has a context and so does your call. Our decision to make this next step was not about me being called into church leadership but first and foremost about us as a family being called into more of God.

So, what about going to Mozambique? Despite being very moved by the faith, sacrifice, changed lives and miracles of Heidi and Rolland's ministry, how could we possibly go there as a young family? Surely, we would just be in the way! What would we do? Where would we fit?

I then saw this thing called Harvest School. It was three months of training at the Iris base in Pemba. Ok, my interest piqued. I clicked on the 'Your questions answered' section and one of the first questions was 'Can I bring my family?'

Yes!! was the bold underlined answer. 'We want you to bring your family' and it went on to specify how they could help etc.

'Babes,' my term of endearment for my wife, 'what do you think about this?' I shouted upstairs. And twenty-four hours later our applications were in.

Now I have never been asked to a movie premier. I have never stepped out of a stretched limo, adjusted my tux and planted expensive Italian leather shoes upon a deep pile scarlet walkway that leads me luxuriously to where I need to be.

But I have experienced God's red carpet.

We stepped onto it on the 31st August 2011 at about 11.35pm. That was the time we received an email telling us we were in. We were Mozambique bound.

Paul talks about *a peace that surpasses all understanding* in his letter to the Philippians. That peace that makes no sense and yet is there anyway, was what we experienced.

We had three weeks to complete on the house sale, which we had been stalling, book flights, see the travel nurse, buy everything we needed for Africa, sell all our furniture and white goods, sort and store what we were keeping, withdraw the children from school and buy home-schooling materials, find someone to look after the dog, pack for three months, and have a miracle with my job which required four weeks' notice.

And yet every day we just seemed to know what needed to be done and how to do it. Jesus made the way. For example: 'Shall we sell the car?' 'Yes!' Phone call that lunchtime from one of Kathryn's brothers. 'Are you selling your car?' He gave us more than we asked for and let us keep it until flight day.

We all needed various injections to equip our weak European immune systems for the wilds of Africa. Kathryn phoned the surgery. 'Sorry, but your departure is too soon for the NHS so you will need to go private.' Ok how much will that cost? 'Over £800.' Ah. I visited the GP, explained our situation (that we were going to work with the poor) and he waived the late request issues and fees!

I wrote a letter to the South East Coast Ambulance Service requesting a short notice resignation. I got the message back that when my line manager spoke to the management team they were so inspired by our adventure and sacrifice that they wanted to offer me a Sabbatical. A Sabbatical that should ordinarily have taken six months to sort and would mean, if nothing opened up post Mozambique, I had a job to come back to.

Red carpet.

And so, we arrived into the heat, smells, excitement and poverty of northern Mozambique 24 days after accepting our Harvest School places.

So maybe now you can understand something of the gravitas that moment held for me as I stepped into my blocks, embraced my 'Olympic' moment, and stared down destiny. Expectation weighed heavily yet wonderfully upon me as Rolland Baker took the microphone. Harvest School and the rest of my life began.

'Here I am Jesus, I am ready, I am open, give me the goods,' was my whispered prayer as Rolland began to speak.

And then it felt more like my life ended. It was well .... a bit weird. A bit seemingly flaky and not life changing or the goods at all. Rolland joked around a bit peppering his talk with slightly amusing and a little controversial one liners. The odd Bible verse did float in but he spent more time pointing his finger at a few people and making a buzzing noise to which they responded like electricity had hit them and I guess were experiencing the Holy Spirit. He even touched one young lady's shoe (she was wearing it) and she fell backwards, seemingly 'filled up.' Everyone was having a great time. There was a glow to the hut. People were smiling with the odd giggle escaping many a lip.

I was fuming.

I did not come all this way, spend all this money and uproot my family for what appeared to all intents and purposes like an off-the-wall 'Holy Spirit Bless Me' time. I could have gone to several churches in the UK for this, with better teaching and a more comfortable chair.

I felt like leaving. I was so angry I wanted to walk out. I felt duped. But I stayed rooted to my plastic garden chair because well... where the heck could I go? I was stuck in the middle of nowhere with this annoying bearded chap. Arrghh!

And suddenly Rolland stopped. He paused and it felt like something shifted. 'God wants to make a point this morning,' he slowly declared. 'Well about time' was my less than happy thought. He continued, undeterred by my flippant thoughts, 'You see nothing here exists because of man. Nothing here as you look around you (Pemba base is huge with a school, orphanage, hospital, workshops, church building, houses etc.) is here because of good ideas or mere hard work. There is only one thing that we rely on, one thing that all of this is run on and without Him this place would shut tomorrow.'

'We only do what Holy Spirit is doing.'

And it felt like a knife went through my heart. In that moment I realised Rolland Baker was totally submitted to Holy Spirit and I wasn't.

He was just doing what Holy Spirit was doing that morning. He wasn't trying to fulfil anyone's expectations, launch the school brilliantly or help us bed in. Later, as I watched his and Heidi's lives, I saw that on other days Holy Spirit was digging latrines, healing the sick, sitting with the needy, teaching pastors and making coffee, and so that's what they did. Here was a man in step with the Spirit, and I was a man in step with my own expectations and wants.

I wanted to be in control. Roland wanted to be under control.

I felt like Isaiah and wanted to cry with him 'Woe to me for I am undone.' And so began my undoing as Holy Spirit, the great surgeon, slowly and consistently cut me to a deeper level than I had yet known and I began to learn to let go, absolutely, unequivocally, of control. Read on

Reflection on Control

By Kathryn

I distinctly remember the evening I knew Matt wouldn't become a teacher!

He and I were driving through the dark to a meeting in 2010 that some good friends had invited us to. At that point our kids were little, so we had got a babysitter and enjoyed the hours' drive of chatting together. Matt was at that stage applying for placements to do teacher training and I thought 'This will be great! If we're both teaching we will have secure jobs, get paid ok and both have school holidays off!'

Suddenly into my spirit dropped the words: 'It's not going to be like that, it's going to be more of a sell-everything-you-have-and-follow-me kind of life!' It was not an audible voice but it was such a clear phrase in my spirit that I welled up and some silent tears rolled down my cheeks. I let go. My Saviour has always had my heart; I would follow.

I knew it wasn't the right time to mention it to Matt and I've learned the kindness of my heavenly Father. He knows me so well, he knows I need preparing in advance for big changes! I might not know exactly what they are going to be but it's like he does a mini operation inside of me so there is room for me to accept the new thing.

So, as we received that prophetic word in the spring of 2011 saying 'The time is now, my child' and the year when God turned our lives upside down began, He had already prepared me to trust. Through the whole experience of selling our house, leaving our jobs, conversing with Highworth Community Church and heading to Africa I felt a deep sense of trusting God that it was going to be ok!

Walking together with Matt through those 8 'wilderness years' in East Preston on the coast, had at times been very hard. There had been a lot of joy with Caleb & Summer arriving (going from 1 child to 3), gardening, DIY, the seaside and new friends, but in the tough things God enabled me to hold onto Him and pray, knowing this 'wilderness' time for Matt especially, would end.

I too, remember the time God's red carpet rolled out before us, 31 Aug 2011, 11:35pm. However, my memory is that while Matt's face looked like a picture of joy that we had been accepted onto the Harvest School in Mozambique... my heart sank! Oh no. It's actually happening, I have to go to Africa!

Still, I chose to trust and God gave us wisdom, joy and unity each day for the next few weeks. However, when we finally arrived in a crumpled heap in a room far too small for the five of us, sweating in the African heat and having just been informed my most useful possession in the coming months would be a stick with which I should retrieve any used toilet roll I had accidentally put down the loo, everything in me thought this must all be a terrible mistake! But there we were. There was no going back. We had left everything to follow Him. All we could do was sit there and sing a worship song, knowing that He knew us better than we knew ourselves!

A day or so later Matt stayed in our room to babysit and I joined in with an evening meeting on the base. As I stopped being a mum, housemate, friend, wife and anything else for a minute, I broke down crying before God, 'I cannot do this!' The thought that I would have to stay here for ten weeks in these conditions where it felt impossible to keep my children and our room safe and clean was more than I could bear.

Once again I so clearly sensed His calm, beautiful words in my spirit: 'Kathryn, I didn't bring you here because you could do it.' His implication that He had brought me here because my own capabilities alone wouldn't be enough to see me through, somehow brought great comfort and hope. And so began my undoing, as, during 'Harvest School,' I let Him have control, stopped resisting, allowed Him to reveal my heart and had the time to fall more deeply in love with Jesus!

Two

Freedom

'You, my brothers and sisters, were called to be free.'

Galatians 5:13

'You have always known God but you haven't always walked with God.' I had been picked out from the dense crowd during a powerful gathering at Marsham St London in 1996 by the preacher and this was how he started a prophetic word for me.

I knew this was God as this simple line encapsulated my life. I cannot ever remember not believing in Him yet there were years when that belief was side-lined and I lived for me.

I was born in Southampton in 1975 and at the tender age of three I became a Pastor's Kid as my mum and dad banded together with some friends who were experiencing new things in the Holy Spirit and started the New Forest Community Church. My early childhood is full of good memories of church walks, picnics, Sunday school and lots and lots of football. My younger brother and I were inseparable and were blessed to be a part of King's School, a Christian school, where speaking in tongues, praying and Jesus were as important as maths and science.

We were a part of the Cornerstone Network of churches, led by Arthur Wallis and Tony Morton. Arthur wrote what was to become one of my favourite books, 'In the Day of Thy Power.' He was a powerhouse in the Spirit and I can remember the mixture of awe and slight fear whenever we got to spend time with him and his lovely wife Eileen.

Bible weeks were a big deal and my dad was involved in running the New Forest Bible week which soon grew into the South and West Bible week. Here, every summer in the rain and occasional sunshine, Jesus was so real. I loved being in the main meetings dwarfed by the thousands of adults worshipping and being allowed to stay up late to hear some amazing preachers. Whether I understood it all or not was unimportant, I could feel it, the presence of God. There was a great honour of leadership back then, nothing silly, but you could feel it and we lived in the blessing of that. I couldn't imagine a better life or one without Jesus. But then we moved.

At the age of eight I went from my beautiful Christian bubble on the south coast to Bridgwater, Somerset - a town with the most pubs per person in the UK, social issues and generally struggling churches. The next 11 years I existed as two different people. One for school and one for home and church. The daily reality of Jesus faded, occasionally punctuated by a Bible week, retreat or visiting speaker. I started to live for me and the results were catastrophic. I rebelled against everything. Smoking, drinking, girls and having a laugh were what I was living for and I kicked out against anything that stood in the way of that. Home life was strained to say the least and school, and then subsequently college, were largely a waste of time.

Deep down I was running away. I wanted life and was trying to find it on my own terms. I would still talk to God. Still speak in tongues whilst walking across the fields to meet my friends so we could go and get drunk in town (crazy!). But it seemed I was on a one-way ticket to nowhere.

In 1994 I joined the British Army and despite being a lazy, partying rebel it felt like maybe my life was coming together. Good career, tick. Girlfriend, tick. Good mates, tick. Very fit and healthy, tick. God? Let's just try and forget about that one. It was all going well until my Achilles tendon gave out during an exercise in basic training and I suddenly found myself back home, on crutches, my faint hopes broken and being swallowed by depression.

Sin caught up with me and everything darkened. I was purposeless and wanted to die, yet knew I wasn't right with God. I did not believe I could change or know how to change.

In half-hearted desperation I went to a meeting at our church one Saturday night in May of 1994. The best night out in town and I went to church! I don't remember what was said but during the preach God put His finger on my life. In a moment I went from vaguely engaged to heart-racing-the-world-has-stopped utterly engaged. I sat before a Holy God with all my mess knowing I was the Prodigal Son and it was time to come home. And I did.

I changed inside. I was torn from the kingdom of darkness into the kingdom of light. I was a new creation - no-one had ever seen this Matt Ford before. All I needed was a place to run. A focus for my passion. A plan for my life.

The starting place came suddenly through a friend of the family who was visiting our church a week or so later. 'Matt can I have a chat with you?' asked Lynn Swart who is a worship leader, teacher and all round lovely person. 'Matt, I have been praying for you and I think you should go to YWAM in Cape Town, South Africa to study and to grow.'

There it was, my inner transformation had an outlet and I took off! (Spiritually and also literally in a plane three months later).

I was in Southern Africa for nearly a year. Learned loads, changed loads and got to do some crazy outreach stuff in Malawi. I saw miracles, received inner healing, inner breakthrough and dug deeper foundations in Christ alone.

Over the following years I went to a residential Spirit filled Bible College. I worked for two brilliant churches, in Winchester and Barking, East London. Here I got to learn how to work God stuff out with people. I learned how to land vision and change, in a way that was sensitive to the past and connected with where people were at. I learned to lead not just with passion but sensitivity and continued to grow and be shaped by encounters with God.

I met and fell in love with someone who loved Jesus more than she loved me. Someone who was willing to say 'yes' to Jesus whatever that meant, and I married my best friend, Kathryn, in 1998.

The previous year I had founded a youth conference called Substance for the Soul with my brother. These ran for six years and would gather 60-80 young people for a few days at least once a year. The vision was simple. Do full on worship, prayer, ministry and teaching. No messing. No kids games or entertainment. No foot off the pedal but to utterly immerse ourselves in Holy Spirit.

They were some of the greatest moments of my life. We would spend hours in worship. One time we ditched all the evening meeting prep just to try and outdo the angels at praising God. Young people worshipped freely, danced, wept, rested and screamed their love for God for hours. Another time we had a whole evening of repentance as God convicted us of our sin and it is one of the closest moments I have ever had to revival. We had times of incredible prophetic ministry, Bible teaching and power encounters and through it all had an absolute blast. It gave us all a window into the future, a 'what was possible' for Church.

Over this whole time I got to travel for Jesus, teaching in Bible schools in the Ukraine and Siberia. I joined teams, and led teams, to India, Columbia, Spain and the USA. I went to a ton of conferences and devoured teaching, Christian books and ministry with an insatiable hunger to know Jesus more.

But then from 2003-2008 I went through the wilderness. I laid down my calling to be led by Holy Spirit into a time of desert and loneliness. I died to so much of my pride and self-reliance in that time and then experienced an incredible season of Holy Spirit encounters as God called me on. At one point the glory of God fell so strongly in our living room, as Kathryn and I prayed, we literally had to hold each other up.

Over those years we welcomed our three children Ethan, Caleb and Summer into the world. From the start we endeavoured to bring them up to know Christ, we often did church at home with little dramas and stories in the lounge and took them to places to experience the presence of God.

I was soon given the opportunity to serve on the leadership team of Arun Church where we worshipped. As a team we guided the church family into a new season and I saw how you can carry forward the good, remain true to your history, yet make changes and embrace new things in a way that is honouring to people and to God.

For nearly 17 years I had pursued Jesus, led, served, prayed, travelled, been filled, studied, worshipped, repented, grown, read books, prophesied, dreamt, discipled, been teachable, received, sacrificed, sat at the feet of great men and women of God, and it had all been good and God had done so much.

Consequently, there in Mozambique in 2011, with Rolland Baker and a very hot sun, the discovery that control still had its subtle, slimy hands on my heart was nothing short of a cataclysmic shock. Somehow through all I had done and desired I wasn't free!

Freedom can be scary

In Mark chapter 10:17-22 we find out how free Jesus is and it's shocking. The disciples are running around checking the windows are locked, the toilet is flushed, and nothing has been left under the beds. Peter, if he's anything like my mum, has the kettle on so they can take a flask and save a few denarii at the Services. James and John are arguing about which was the quickest route to the capital and how best to avoid the roadworks and the average speed check cameras leading up to the Sheep Gate.

Amidst the normal frantic activity that any group encounters when setting out on a journey, a wealthy young man runs up, falls to his knees before Jesus and blurts out a stunning question:

'Good teacher, what must I do to inherit eternal life?' (vs 17)

And there it is on a plate. I've had a couple of people come up to me and ask me for a light, once someone asked to borrow my phone and I seem to recall a plea from a harassed pensioner clutching an empty lead asking if I'd seen their little dog?' But no-one has ever approached me out of the blue and hit me with one of the biggest questions out there.

And so this beautiful and tragic scene unfolds. Without missing a beat, Jesus challenges him with the commandments, with the core issues of how you should live your life before God. *'All these I have done since I was a boy,'* was the reply. Wow! This guy not only is searching for the truth but has a history of serious and passionate response to what he has been told. Sign him up! And it's not just me.

'Jesus looked at him and loved him' (vs 21).

So, here's the next Apostle surely or at least put him on the substitutes bench in case that funny-looking Judas guy doesn't work out. This man is humble (he's on his knees), serious, has a history of discipline, is searching for the truth and loved in an encounter with Jesus.

Instead Jesus turns it up a notch, or a few, and in the same verse says: *'One thing you lack, go sell everything you have... and come follow me.'*

Sharp intake of breath. That is pretty out there, especially by today's standards of what it means to be a Christian. But still, he is offered the opportunity of a lifetime - Jesus has chosen him to be part of the team! However, the young man's face drops, his shoulders slump and he turns and leaves. Unfortunately, he was looking for more he could achieve, not give up, and he can't let go of his great wealth. It's one ask too far and he departs crestfallen.

And Jesus lets him go. This guy is allowed to walk away. I would have gone after him. Toned down the commitment (who of us has done what Jesus asked of him?) encouraged him to tithe or at least do an Alpha Course. Jesus says nothing. Does nothing. The one who leaves the 99 lets this passionate, but compromised, young guy go.

Unfortunately for us this is not an isolated incident. Jesus constantly goes off script, changes the goal posts and follows no pattern or ordered system. It turns out Christ is a serial freedom perpetrator.

In John 11, He delays his visit to the dying Lazarus causing others the pain of loss and in John 4 He abandons a full-scale revival in Samaria. He raises a widow's son in Luke 7 without even being asked yet plays hard to get despite the cries of the Canaanite woman in Matthew 15. In John 2 he kicks miracles off 'before his time', to save the bride and grooms blushes, yet does nothing when asked for a miracle by the religious leaders in Matthew 16. Jesus wipes out an entire farmer's herd to set one demon possessed man free in Mark 5, yet sets countless others free from demonic oppression, without any loss to their neighbour's income streams. And surely, in one of the greatest freedom offenses in history, Judas is still allowed access to the money, to not only follow Christ but to be one of the select few apostles despite his wayward heart, thieving hands and penchant for demonic manipulation.

Jesus constantly and consistently exhibited a level of freedom from what makes sense, what was the done thing, how things had been done, people's expectations, others needs or hopes and to be frank, reason itself.

Jesus came to show us the Father to reveal what God is really like. *'If you have seen me you've seen the Father'* (John 14:9) was Jesus' often quoted and stunning statement. If you want to know what God is like look at Jesus. And what we see is freedom. A freedom that is both compelling and scary. God is totally free. He is freedom itself and if we are not free we are not like Him.

Jesus describes the lifestyle of those who are born again to a befuddled Nicodemus in John chapter 3. *'The wind blows wherever it pleases. You hear its sound, but you cannot tell where it comes from or where it is going. So it is with everyone born of the Spirit.'* (vs 8).

What a picture of freedom. Born and moving like the wind, effective and experienced, yet never constrained, understood or put in a box. This is an attractive and frightening picture of what it is to really walk with the Holy Spirit, and it is utterly free of control.

To be free of control sounds like great news and something we would all easily align with. We universally dislike people who are 'controlling', yet when we experience even a little loss of power, we realize how much we want to control everything.

Impotent

Being in Pemba Mozambique with Iris Global had been an invitation to learn from the poor. I hadn't realised that meant experiencing what it is like to be poor! Being poor means you have zero power and therefore zero control.

It was maybe week three and I turned on the kitchen tap to be met with a pathetic trickle of dirty water that quickly became a drip and then disappeared. The water was out. And no one could tell me when it would come back on. It could be an hour, or could be a week, or as someone remarked rather blasé (in my opinion) 'that could be it for the next two months!' There was no one to phone and no one to blame. It just was.

I think at that time we went ten days with no running water. Our supplies were used up within a few days despite my super frugal 500ml showers, and we faced the hot trek to the well and the hotter trek back, where we discovered how heavy water is. Health deteriorated as we had to use open latrines as the toilets were unflushable and 'normal' things like washing up and mopping floors became a luxury. To make matters worse the electricity then decided not to be around for a few days which meant no fridge, lights or fans for the sweltering nights.

And there was me. Dad. The one who runs to get the car when everyone is tired, who eats up the buffet food the kids no longer want to save embarrassment, and is wired to protect, keep safe and provide for his family. And I was powerless. Anger, worry, frustration had to be let go of and I was resigned to meet each day as it came, trying my best and rolling with the punches. It was a simple, profound and life altering lesson.

Surely, the ridiculous levels of stress and anxiety in our society spew from a fount of inner belief that life can be controlled but the experience that it can't. Yet, instead of recognising this and adjusting our beliefs, we build a bigger insurance wall, dig ever deeper, fight harder and/or take some medication to maintain the bubble.

The deception of control is that we can't actually control anything.

We desperately want life to happen our way, to win. We want to always have enough energy so we can cope, have enough money in the bank to cover any possible future emergency or enough time to complete what needs doing. My experience often in prayer ministry is people come for prayer as a last resort when the problems and challenges have reached a point that is now beyond their control. We want God to control life or at least give it the appearance and safety of control. We want Him to keep us cotton wool safe, never let us grapple with doubts or have to persevere through trials. We want Him to rescue us quickly from every problem, provide beforehand for every need and make sure we never get a parking fine.

We don't want freedom; we want control.

We all want to control our children because we want to limit their risk, the risk of them being hurt, of failing, of making the same mistakes we did. We want to control our churches because we want them to do well, we want people to grow, find Jesus and change the world or at least be happy. But control will always take us ultimately in the other direction and our lives end up being a testimony not of freedom but to the chains of fear, worry, desire for financial security, boundaries, compartmentalisation and apathy. Our lives are not witnesses to the freedom that God lives.

Blessed are the poor

A couple of weeks after the water incident in Mozambique, I met a man when visiting the sick in the local hospital who showed me freedom. He had had to give up his job to travel here from a village some distance away because his young daughter was dying of malaria. In his arms he held his recently born son and he told us how his wife had died giving birth to him. And yet, through the tears and hopelessness, he told us he was trusting Jesus.

His life was completely out of control. He had no power and I struggled to find words of comfort or hope. Yet he still trusted. The poor know how to move with the ebbs and flows of life. They know it is uncontrollable and they know how to smile, how to weep and how to keep moving in the midst of its complexities.

'Blessed are the poor in spirit, for theirs is the kingdom of heaven,'
(Matthew 5:3)

That man's story doesn't look like our "abundant life and options available -'like the wind'" idea of freedom. Yet, I knew in the brief moments I spent with him, that he was way freer than I was. He was resting in God, despite the pain and the unknown, whereas I kicked against everything that got in my way and blamed God when things didn't turn out right. I want God to steer, nudge and sometimes outright push me into the right course. He is very kind, He can do anything, but He is also completely free.

To have power and not control is to be like God.

I cannot emphasise the sheer transformation this freedom has had upon my life, to not control and let God work. Here's a couple of examples:

Leadership

One of my colleagues at church thought and processed ideas differently to me. We were different characters with different gifts but needed to work together. I was struggling so I talked to God about it, 'How could we ever work together Lord?' I was sat there thinking about how my colleague probably needed to change etc. when I felt a crazy freedom nudge 'Son I want you to agree with and support any idea or advice they have.'

Living in freedom means living in obedience, so despite my reservations and God's advice seeming to fly in the face of my perspective on leadership, I went with it, letting go of my agenda, willing to change my ideas and trust in God.

So if my colleague shared an idea I supported it. If they shared some cautionary thoughts, I listened. If they challenged, I took it to heart. And God did something wonderful. I began to value them. See them. Actually seek out their advice. God drew our hearts together and I discovered we weren't really different. We were not going after conflicting plans. We were looking at exactly the same thing, with exactly the same hope and passion, just from a different perspective.

For a couple of years we would meet up at least every couple of weeks for a coffee and I would pour out my heart and they theirs. They taught me to think differently and see more fully.

I still miss their 'difference' today.

Vision

In late spring 2015, Kathryn and I were at a church members meeting, to answer questions on a proposal for three months unpaid leave to go to Cambodia.

The meetings atmosphere held a full range of emotions - you could feel the interest, concern, questions and fears, all wrapped up with more than a little tension. I could feel my heart wanting to race and fought to not give into any stress and instead be what everyone needed me to be that night. To be free.

It had started as a realisation of our own lack. Maybe eight months before we had hit the bottom. We were not depressed or discouraged, just keenly aware of how bogged down we had become with the thousand little details of western church life. We were aware that our God given vision to minister as a family, to be a hub together of worship and prayer wasn't happening. We were quickly getting stuck in a maintenance lifestyle and knew we had lost passion, faith and courage so we had sought after a radical response.

Your own heart is a gate. God wants to pour His Spirit through our lives, but the condition of our hearts limits what God can do. For the gate to be open requires faith, trust, hope and passion. We knew our hearts, our gates, needed to be swung wide again so going and serving Iris Cambodia for three months was what we believed was the solution. It was not a retreat but an advance. Three months of living simply, with the poor and with fired up missionaries. Three months of learning and letting God work in our hearts.

We were utterly convinced this was God. We felt His hand on the whole thing and believed the best possible thing for our hearts, our future ministry and the local church we were serving, was for us to go. Now to convince everyone else.

I was aware there were a host of reasonable and valid responses to our request. We knew it brought up questions of commitment 'You said God had called you here.' We knew it probably didn't make sense to a lot of people, 'You're three years into a calling and now you want out?' We knew it wasn't in my contract, we knew there were care filled questions of what it would mean for our children's education. Some people would feel it wasn't fair - they didn't get to just shoot off on a God whim - and some would conclude we had an eye on greener grass.

But I knew it was God.

Your conviction is never a hammer to smash everything that stands in your way. Knowing God has called you to something should set you free. If it really is His will then you don't need to force, cajole, convince or control, you can let go and let God.

So, my preparation for all those questions was not constructing brilliant answers, or strategising an impassioned vision. I knew all I could bring to that meeting was freedom. I knew I had to go willing to lose my job. Willing to not please everyone. Willing to be honest.

Freedom begets freedom. I was not there to convince everyone but honour them where they were and create the space where we could all process together. What could have been confrontational became invitational. Freedom allowed us to open the door for the church to join us spiritually on our adventure and you can read about some of what happened and the impact it had upon us in later chapters.

Some deeper magic

Freedom has affected everything. How I parent, who we are as a family, how I lead and what I believe a local church should be like. Letting go of control and trying to walk in the freedom of God has influenced everything in this book, but here are some specific things that I can see have flowed from this revelation.

Firstly, there is no formula. For anything. Despite a whole ton of 'How to' books, whether on family, parenting, small groups, worship teams, leadership models etc. etc. etc. there really, really is no formula. Please, please stop looking. You are the only you on the planet. Your family is the only family with this specific set of people in it. Your church is the only one like it. We are unique! It is vital that we hear from others about their successes and or failures, and we must search, look and study in order to change. But, it is never to copy or try and replicate. Instead these things should push us deeper into Jesus, reveal gaps in our understanding that we then get filled by Christ, and shake us out of mediocrity or compromise, to find new love and passion in Him. The things in this book are seeds to plant in your relationship with Jesus, not scripts to follow.

Secondly, there are no guarantees. Christ called everyone but controlled no one. I desperately want my children to follow Jesus. I live, and give, that my church family would be fruitful and blessed but I, like Jesus, choose zero control over those things. Freedom keeps me there, it keeps me loving, hoping, praying and serving, though I know church can implode at the drop of a hat (I have seen it happen before) and my children may choose to reject Christ.

Thirdly, freedom releases Wisdom. Jesus was questioned by the greatest minds of His nation, men intent on catching him out, devising questions they viewed as theological traps, but He was uncatchable. His answers were staggering. His ability to not only answer well, but in such a way as to reveal hearts and lay bare misconception, flowed from freedom. I believe I have experienced a little something of this. Jesus hadn't secretly swotted up on apologetics or assigned a special angelic team to an 'answering the toughest questions on the planet' focus group. He was free. When the world and people have nothing on you, when all you do is to please the Father and you are unconcerned, in a caring way, about how people respond to you, then you can know real in-the-moment wisdom.

Fourthly, freedom helps us to deal brilliantly with hurts and with failures. Most Christians get really free when they get saved but then hit a wall. They get hurt by other Christians or by the church. If you have been part of a church for more than five years or probably even less, it is likely someone, or something has hurt you. The 'people of love' and the 'house of love' is the hardest and most confusing place to get hurt. I have been let down, betrayed, failed, insulted, blanked, criticised, judged, controlled, manipulated and overlooked and that was just this last week! (Joke). Seriously though my church experience hasn't been that bad, but I have experienced all of the above and more. Freedom pushes me to not let these experiences be shaping forces in my life. Freedom keeps me forgiving, loving back, getting healed and keeps me still giving the gift of trust. Once you have really tasted and really understood freedom, you won't let anything enslave you again.

In the UK we say 'once bitten twice shy.' Basically, if something goes wrong be ultra-cautious and keep yourself safe so it doesn't ever happen again. We have all failed at something and been very tempted to never do that again. That is the world's kingdom, not Christ's. I fail. The issue is not desperately trying to avoid failure but instead, desperately avoiding our freedom getting enslaved by our failures.

You *will* fail. Settle in your heart today that when you do you won't let fear, guilt or condemnation in the door and instead humbly repent and let Christ, and those who love you, restore you. When I finally lift my head after failing (and I am slowly getting quicker at lifting it), every single time I find the Christ of John chapter 21 gently and firmly calling me to try and to trust again. Yes, learn from your mistakes, yes, don't be an idiot, but ultimately we just have to get healed up and step out again. That is to live free.

And finally freedom has taught me responsibility. The profound mystery with God's freedom is that it actually makes you more responsible not less. Freedom and responsibility are not two conflicting values. Apologies to those who were reading this chapter as some divine thumbs up to a carefree existence divested of all obligation and duty. That's the freedom our society craves, the desire to live unrestrained and unchecked, to not be held back by anyone, to be free of someone else's accountability and to have the right to do whatever we feel we want, without anyone telling us what we can or cannot do. It wants to be free of the past, free of institution and free to choose. This is a warped, selfish understanding of something far greater. Freedom, for Jesus, enabled Him to be the most responsible person that has ever walked on planet earth.

More on responsibility

In Luke 8 Jesus is hurrying to a dying girl when He stops because in the midst of the crowd someone has touched the hem of His garment. In Matthew 14 Jesus withdraws to mourn the loss of His friend John, but then allows thousands of people to not only interrupt, but stay, and then provides for them supernaturally. Weak and hungry in Luke 4, Jesus overcomes the wiles of Satan himself by simply trusting in the Scriptures, walking through that challenge as one of us, using no divine power as an example we can follow. Because He is free, Jesus puts His health on the line and breaks the Levitical law in Matthew 8 touching and healing a leper. In Mark 7 and Matthew 8, Jesus works miracles and endorses 'great faith' on those outside the covenant. In Luke 23, Jesus turns aside from literally saving the world to love a criminal, permitting the simplest step of faith to matter. Time and again His 'handpicked' disciples, those the Father had given Him responsibility for, fail to understand what's going on, say the wrong thing or just plain fail to believe, yet Freedom means Jesus never rejects them, is never embarrassed or ashamed of them and keeps trusting that they are the right men for the job.

And in the greatest freedom act of all time, Christ lets humans arrest, accuse, beat, strip, humiliate and nail Him to a cross. Taking responsibility for their sin and ours, even though He was blameless and at a word ten thousand angels could have been at His side.

True freedom actually makes you more responsible!

Freedom meant Jesus could act differently and actually serve and love a broken world. Jesus lived a perfect life. He never ever put a foot or a word wrong. He only did what He saw the Father doing (John 15:19), how crazy free and crazy responsible is that! Freedom meant Jesus could respond to the Father and the Father alone. Freedom meant He was never swayed by people, situations or even His own ideas. That's true responsibility.

Freedom is living without trying to control anything, even for good, and constantly laying your own agenda at the feet of Jesus.

How do we find the power to stay free? How does the cross stay active in my life beyond my conversion? It's an authority issue; so read on.

Reflection on Freedom

By Kathryn

I want to share a story with you about a lady called Grace*. It was on my birthday in Dec 2013. As a family we were on a mission trip in Cambodia for three weeks. Our wonderful friends Steve & Mollie asked if we'd like them to babysit so we could go out for a meal together! We realised what we'd much rather do was go on an adventure with God! Mollie spoke the local language and so we asked her to come with us. We prayed, asked God to lead us, left Steve watching the kids and set off. After having one chance to chat and pray with a girl in the central tourist area we found a tuk tuk and asked the driver to take us to the "girlie bars". He looked surprised and told us it was far away but he set off for the red light district. We left the lights of the tourist area and headed into dark streets. We had no clue where we were going and realised none of us had a working mobile phone on us! We prayed again and trusted God. We let go of control and chose to freely follow the wind of Holy Spirit.

Finally we reached a street full of 'girlie bars', randomly picked a girl out of a line-up at the entrance to one and sat down to have a drink and chat with her. Grace told us how her husband had gone to Thailand to look for work, she was here with the three kids and no way to earn money. This job was the best way she could find. She hated it and would never tell her husband. She felt lost and longed for a different life. We were able to spend that time sharing with her how much God loved her and that she was valuable to Him. We invited her to a gospel music festival our team were doing the next night. We were unsure if she would come, could she spare the time away from work? Do you know what? Grace was the first to arrive! She brought her brother and his wife, sat near the front, took everything in and was amongst the first to go to the front and receive Jesus into her life at the end!

That night wasn't random at all! She had been used and not experienced real love. But Grace mattered so much to God that he sent three ordinary English people from thousands of miles away to go out into the darkness, to her bar, pick her out and let her know she mattered!

Whenever I reflect on that story I am so delighted and privileged that God chose to use us. But the journey to the freedom of that night came through many small, daily, choices. God has worked in my heart (especially since Mozambique) to help me let go of things like having the house perfectly tidy or worrying if the carpet is hoovered before friends come round. Not trying to do too much or be a superhuman mum who has all the right things ready for their child's next school day! I have to let go of control again anytime Matt decides to help out with the laundry pile by tipping clothes everywhere and doing an 'un-colour-coordinated' load of washing!

Daily freedom choices about parenting are common and I started learning one sleepless night when baby Ethan was a few weeks old (and no-one else's baby advice was working), that Holy Spirit is a genius at knowing our children and what to do better than anybody! I remember a few stressful incidents in Mozambique when one of our children was not coping with the environment and another mum's child had come off worse! All I wanted to do was run away and hide. Worldly wisdom told me to reproach and punish our child whilst hiding with shame as their behaviour reflected me. But, as we desperately asked God what to do he began to teach us to ask for specific keys in order to live free with our children, help them and not just get angry or stressed with them. In different seasons these "keys" will be different for each child but they are whatever God leads us to do or say even when it is unexpected. The key in that situation was to start by coming alongside them and understanding from their perspective why they felt angry.

God says 'my ways are not your ways' and He is constantly having to help me embed these freedom lessons. Teaching me to have freedom to sell the house that we had spent lots of money rebuilding and renovating exactly as we wanted it to, then squeeze our family into a few square feet in Mozambique. Learning to have freedom to leave the heat of Africa and the joyful, amazing, open heaven environment that Iris hosts, to return to the country of our missionary calling in the sub-zero winter of 2015/16. To have no fixed abode, to live in a caravan and be so aware of England's spiritual "greyness". Growing freedom to have grace, patience and trust when we first moved to Highworth and were sharing a house with kind friends for much longer than any of us expected. (I'm sure they had to have even more grace!) Unexpected freedom to then rent a seven bedroom house where the joy of many guests to encourage in God also meant more floors to sweep and beds to change. Current freedom to live in a cheap flat with simple rooms that we needed and not be able to host guests or have a garden.

Freedom was needed when I felt God urging me to take a team of ladies from our Highworth church to Mexico on a mission trip with Amy Lancaster and WeWillGo. Leaving the kids and Matt for 12 days was not an easy choice but what I learnt from her in that time impacted me forever! I had to let go of controlling the family environment for that time, trust that Matt had this and that God would incredibly use this time. I need to ask God to help me live free every day, not controlling but aiming to be led by Him.

not her real name.

Three

Authority

'Then Jesus came to them and said, "All authority in heaven and on earth has been given to me. Therefore go.'

Matthew 28:18-19

It felt like they were on the edge of breakthrough and on this important night the disciples would have wanted everything to be perfect. It was the great feast of Passover and we find this event in John chapter 13.

Things had been building and months of ministry in the countryside seemed to be reaching a climax. Finally, here in Zion, Jerusalem, the centre of faith, they were bringing this good news of God's Kingdom. The atmosphere was electric. Everyone had heard about their friend from Bethany coming back to life, called out of the tomb no less, and they had become the talk of the town! Change was in the air. The Temple system had quite literally been upturned and Christ had made great prophetic or declarations. These had led to inevitable confrontations with the religious leaders, but all had left tails between their legs, their questions pulled to pieces and incredible teaching laying them bare.

And now they got to celebrate Passover, remembering the salvation God brought to Israel all those years ago and it felt more relevant, more significant than ever before.

All the preparations had been made, instructions followed to the letter and now with the smell of roasting meat and bitter herbs they realised their mistake. As they sat there ready to take their seats, staring at their soiled feet and waiting for the Jewish version of washing your hands before dinner, the realisation that they had all forgotten to organise a basic duty hit them.

They all looked at each other. Some with accusing eyes, 'You should've thought of this,' others sheepishly hoping someone else would take a bit of responsibility and go find a slave. No one wanted to catch Jesus' eyes. Awkward.

And then the master stands, takes off His robe, wraps a towel around his waist and begins to do the lowest thing imaginable. He washes their dusty, sweaty and smelly feet. Here the creator of the universe gently cleanses the most offensive and base part of their bodies.

With this simple gesture, Jesus ushers in the most remarkable weekend in the world's history. A weekend where the authority of His Kingdom will triumph over the powers of darkness. And it came in a way utterly foreign to our understanding. This is authority like we have never seen before which starts and flows from an insight John shares: *'Jesus knew that the Father had put all things under his power, and that he had come from God and was returning to God.' (John 13:3)*

He washes their feet because He knows who He is.

Authority is what enables us to walk in true Christ-like freedom. Authority is the answer to the tension between control and anarchy. Only your true identity in Christ will release the authority of God in your life.

In that moment in the Upper Room the disciples witnessed the wonder of really knowing your identity, the unearthly power of God. They were there, present when leadership was turned on its head and nothing would be the same again. My own personal witness however, came over a Starbucks Christmas blend coffee.

It was maybe 8am and we were on mission to an isolated village in Mozambique. Tired from hours of travel and a wonderful but exhausting outreach the previous day, the team and I were milling around a large open courtyard and already seeking respite from the heat of the rising sun.

I remember being hungry and thirsty and wondering who would provide some much needed breakfast. Glancing past those gathered in the crowded shade I saw a lady kneeling on the hard packed earth by the open fire nursing five battered cafetieres. Heidi Baker was making me a coffee. Heidi who is CEO of Iris Global, holds a PHD in Theology from Kings College, London and is the author of several bestsellers. Heidi Baker, who people in the west flocked to hear, who had seen more miracles than I can count, planted hundreds of churches and counted the cost over years of ministry, was there, where I knew Jesus would be. Happily serving. Content in the lowest place.

True power is meek

I was listening recently to someone preach a message on the power of God. It was an encouragement into the miraculous, but a verse they quoted struck me like never before: *And having disarmed the powers and authorities, he made a public spectacle of them, triumphing over them by the cross. (Colossians 2:15)*

They were reading the verses in terms of victory, but I was hit by the fact that victory looked like failure. It looked like Jesus' weakness. It was Christ taking it and taking it again. It was meekness and humility. This broken bleeding man, seemingly without power, future or hope, was a public spectacle of God's authority disarming the enemy's authority.

Washing the disciples' feet. Hanging meekly nailed to a cross. This was not God beating the enemy into submission, it was Him pulling the rug from under his feet. A new authority broke out upon creation that weekend. An authority that would never again be upturned and guaranteed a new heaven and earth and the ending of death itself. And it came low, meek, humble, in weakness, resting in the utter confidence of knowing who He really was.

This is how He works - always.

I want authority in my life. Authority is the difference between merely following Jesus and being like Jesus. I want to see what the disciples saw, when they were given His authority (Matthew 10:1) to beat back the enemy, dispel darkness, crush sickness and build the Kingdom and therefore God's family. But authority really is rather different according to God.

The Kingdom of God

I think to grasp all this we have to understand, what I personally believe, is the key message of the Bible. The Kingdom of God.

I am indebted to my time way back in 1995/6 with the staff and lecturers at King's Bible College. They instilled in me a passion and understanding of the Kingdom that was both biblical and experiential (I have lived it). The Kingdom was the great theme of my studies that year, and the following was particularly shaped by one lecturer, Bryan Watts, and the teaching from his book *Treasure in the Field (Imogen Resources 1995)*. Here's a little of what I gleaned:

To really understand authority, we need to understand the Kingdom of God. The Kingdom is not a health club where you pay a fee to procure a membership. It is a culture of rule, a realm in which this rule is experienced, and at its centre, a King on a throne. Matthew's gospel talks about the Kingdom of Heaven. This is exactly the same as the Kingdom of God; it was Matthew being sensitive to his mainly Jewish audience who would not write the name of God.

In the expansive and wildly descriptive book of Revelation, before we get dragons, scrolls, pale horses, bowls, wrath, trumpets, whores and a whole lot of blood and fire, at its opening in Chapter 4, before everything else, John sees the Throne of the Universe and someone is sitting upon it (verse 2)! It's the most important thing to grasp, if we are to have any chance of understanding the apocalyptic prophecy and it is also a verse that sits at the core of our faith.

The Kingdom of God starts with the Throne and He who sits upon it. This is the origin, the source of the Kingdom and all else flows from this.

The Lord reigns, He is robed in majesty, the Lord is robed in majesty and is armed with strength. The world is firmly established; it cannot be moved. Your throne was established long ago; you are from all eternity. (Psalm 93: 1-2)

Yours, O LORD, is the greatness and the power and the glory and the victory and the majesty, indeed everything that is in the heavens and the earth; Yours is the dominion, O LORD, and You exalt Yourself as head over all. (1 Chronicles 29:11)

In our modern turbulent world, where nations are largely governed by the dramatic rise and fall of political parties and their often-questionable leaders, we fail to grasp the true power and authority of thrones and kingship. Even at an earthly human level, past kings (and queens) wielded power and authority beyond anything we have experienced, and John sees THE King. Eternal, on a throne in Heaven. The impact and significance of this is astounding.

The King is untouchable, it is impossible to successfully challenge our God. God's throne remains unaffected by events on earth. It is so far above all, that God is without rival, and nothing here, can change what is there. There is no rule, authority, power or dominion which can touch it. Its nature is such that it cannot be threatened. God's throne is universal. It is absolute. It is complete. It is the one thing in the whole universe that is so fixed that everything else revolves around it.

His throne is the glue that makes a universe rather than a multiverse.

'Christ is the visible image of the invisible God. He existed before anything was created and is supreme over all creation, for through him God created everything in the heavenly realms and on earth. He made the things we can see and the things we can't see— such as thrones, kingdoms, rulers, and authorities in the unseen world. Everything was created through him and for him. He existed before anything else, and he holds all creation together. Christ is also the head of the church, which is his body, He is the beginning, supreme over all who rise from the dead. So he is first in everything.' (Colossians 1:15)

God is on the Throne of the universe and there is no moving Him!

This means we are not stuck in some epic Hollywood-esque movie. We are not a small, ragtag group of 'heroes' fighting against a seemingly insurmountable and superior force. History is not God striving to overcome a wayward universe. The ending is not that good triumphs but only just, and against the run of play!

No, the good news is the King is on the throne! History is the masterful creative handiwork of a God whose throne is eternally secure. Calvary was not a last-ditch response to the problem of sin, no, the Lamb was slain from the foundation of the world (Revelation 13:8).

History really is His story.

The Kingdom of God is the great theme of the New Testament. John the Baptist heralds in the coming Messiah with the cry 'the Kingdom of God is at hand!' Jesus' ministry was either teachings about the Kingdom of God or great demonstrations of Kingdom power and kindness. After conquering death, Christ spends his last 40 days on earth teaching His disciples the things of the Kingdom (Acts 1:3), and in the last verse of the book of Acts we find the Apostle Paul choosing to spend his final moments preaching the Kingdom of God. All the other New Testament happenings, teachings, events and miracles are just the impact of this Kingdom on the advance.

What is it?

Super. So, we know the Kingdom flows from an unshakeable throne and a King who rules absolutely, but what is it? What is the Kingdom of God?

Simply put, it is the government of God. This has two aspects, Realm and Rule. We need to understand both of these. Realm is the domain, the area or place over which God's government is exercised. The Rule (or dominion) describes God's activities in governing.

For example, King David's Realm was Judah and Israel, this was the geographic area over which he was king. His Rule was what happened in that area, the level of justice, the opportunities, the values and level of safety etc. It was what a citizen experienced living in that realm. Interestingly, Queen Elizabeth II has a realm but no rule. Her realm is the United Kingdom, but she has no authority or power over its rule, over what happens in it.

When Jesus stood in the Synagogue at Nazareth and declared His manifesto by reading from the prophet Isaiah (Luke 4:18-19), He was describing the rule of God. This is what a citizen of the Kingdom of God would experience and be a part of:

- The poor receive good news
- The broken hearted are bound up and healed
- Captives are set free
- Release from darkness for prisoners
- Favour upon God's people
- Vengeance upon all that is evil and stands against God
- Comfort for those who mourn
- Provision for those who grieve

It is a rule that replaces ashes with beauty, mourning with gladness and a spirit of despair with a garment of praise. This is what happens in the Kingdom of God!

So, if this is what the rule is like, where does this rule happen? Where is the realm of God's Kingdom?

'Then Jesus said to His disciples, "If anyone wishes to come after me, he must deny himself, and take up his cross and follow me. For whoever wishes to save his life will lose it; but whoever loses his life for my sake will find it." (Matthew 16:24-25)'

The realm is in the lives of everyone who bows the knee to Christ. When you say 'yes' to Jesus, the Kingdom comes! This is why the cry of the gospels is 'Repent!' Stop going your way and go His way because the Kingdom of God is at hand.

Tying this all together: authority is the power and the right of an enthroned God to extend His rule and reign on the Earth, which is really, really, really good.

This Kingdom comes, this authority is established and built on a submissive attitude toward the throne. Before we have any hope of understanding authority, we have to understand submission to the King. Sub mission, to put your agenda, likes, wants, ideas and will underneath Christ's agenda, wants, likes, ideas and will. We are all called to this life of submission, it's called Christianity.

Knees bent

To take up your cross is to submit. To be crucified with Christ is to submit. To repent; literally change direction from your way to His; is to submit.

To lead is to be in greater submission than those you are leading. If I am to successfully be a leader of Highworth Community Church, I need to be the most submitted person in the room. Leadership without submission always fails. It has been my experience that the further you journey in leadership, it becomes less and less about your ideas and vision, and more about helping everyone else realise theirs, and through it all realise Christ's.

You cannot lead where you have not been.

To be a parent is to be a leader. The issue then as with any leadership position in the Kingdom, is how do you lead? What does submitted leadership look like?

In Mark chapter 10:42-44 it says, regarding the disciples, those who had submitted to following Him, that *'Jesus called them together and said, "You know that those who are regarded as rulers of the Gentiles lord it over them, and their high officials exercise authority over them. Not so with you. Instead, whoever wants to become great among you must be your servant, and whoever wants to be first must be a slave of all."*

Here Jesus shares how authority works where He rules and reigns. This is in direct contrast to how authority works where man and sinful humans rule and reign. The world's power works through being 'over' others. The leader is more important than those under them, and position is gained by lifting yourself up and keeping others in their place. They have the power to decide what those below them should and shouldn't do, and they generally work towards a goal exerting that power to achieve the target. It's always a pyramidal structure with control at its heart. This control can easily become oppressive, squashing others or silencing certain voices in order to get your way.

Many churches, ministries and families have been run on this system for generations. Leaders should be obeyed; parents should be honoured, and their wishes enforced. People can work within this system with a good heart and in love, but it never ends up looking like the leadership, nor therefore the authority, that Christ wanted us to express. It's so important that we realise this is authority, but not God's authority. It's a system of government outside of the Kingdom. Our problem is we are so wired to interpret leadership and authority within this style that we express it without thinking, and those of us who have been hurt by Christian leadership end up rejecting the idea of authority and submission altogether.

Interestingly, we have seen the consistent and increasing breakdown of this way of leadership and authority in the world over the last few decades. Respect and honour for leaders has disappeared. Institution has been rejected, and people are throwing off the shackles of an authority that is viewed and experienced as oppressive and burdensome. Anything older or traditional, whether person or organisation, is treated with a growing contempt by younger generations, and there is a growing tide pushing for a perceived freedom where everyone has a choice, a voice and freedom. But it is an empty, hyped unreality. What an amazing opportunity we all have to reveal a heavenly leadership and Kingdom authority that goes low, instead of over!

Parents = leaders

And it starts in the home. To be a parent is to be a leader. To lead well we have to be submitted. Whatever books we read, techniques we glean from YouTube or courses we attend, if we are not more submitted to Jesus than our children are, our authority will always be skewed by the world. It will result in a parenting authority that is based on fear. If a parent's wishes are not obeyed, whether it's tidying your room or being back by 9pm, then there will be consequences. If a child doesn't do x, y or z then there will be punishments like sitting on the step, a reduction in pocket money or being grounded. The child's obedience is based on the fear of punishment. This doesn't mean there are not repercussions for disobedience, the Bible is clear on that, but it's an authority based on punishment and on control, not submission and freedom.

We were standing outside our house a couple of years ago, saying goodbye to some good friends. We live in a flat with a communal car park that runs down to a busy road. Their oldest child, a rather full of beans toddler, suddenly took off down the side of our house towards the road and danger. Dad shouted for him to 'stop' and 'come back' but nothing happened. Dad's voice rose in volume and demand, but still two stubby little legs propelled said child away from safety. It was only a mad rush after him that halted his progress, and I was left bewildered at what these days is a very common scene. A complete lack of obedience in children.

Now before you fear I am about to go all Victorian, it wasn't the lack of obedience per se that bothered me, but the absence of authority. Dad's words carried no weight, which nearly resulted in a terrible accident. Authority keeps people safe. We have probably all experienced the substitute teacher whose class descends into chaos, and despite them shouting at the top of their voice, order is not resumed. Conversely, we have all experienced the calm, measured voice of a teacher in command, and the effect that voice has to instil order.

Authority becomes the foundation for freedom, not a barrier to its fulfilment.

When you know who you are as a much-loved child of God; when you carry no shame or regret and are comfortable with your own frailties and weakness; when you know what you are and are not gifted at, but see neither as a divine tick or a disqualification; when you have a clear vision of your calling and walk it out, undemanding and free of control, you discover authority based on your relationship to the Throne and not people. You discover an authority rooted in an identity that releases identity.

'All authority has been given to me - go!' To paraphrase the Son of God: 'I know who I am; better, kinder and holier than anyone who ever has, or will, walk this earth, so therefore I release you to go and be the same.'

I was sat in our very nice and very local coffee house, which is more like a home than a shop, TT Linnets (unashamed plug, it's awesome), with Andrew Price who is part of our church oversight and a great friend. We were conspiring over a leadership training school we were going to trial at HCC and he asked me, 'What do you want to achieve? What is the one thing you want the students to come away with?' A hundred lovely Christian things cascaded through my mind, but like a lens coming into focus, one word jumped out at me in bold and underlined. 'Authority,' I blurted out.

The desperate need in our generation is Christians to lead, wherever they are, by going low and washing feet, utterly convinced of their identity in Christ.

In the home

As a parent, my realm (where I serve) is my household, and the rule is what those living in that household experience and live in.

One of the major experiences of living in the realm of the kingdom is safety. I am now held in the arms of one more powerful than me. I am hidden with Christ in God (Colossians 3), my future and my soul untouchable. Worry and fear are things I no longer need to live with. God is now for me, so who can be against me (Romans 8)! I am not talking about a cotton wool safety, I am talking about a combative, active safety - the fearing no evil, even in the valley of the shadow of death type safety, the safety that experiences the table laid before me in the presence of my enemies (Psalm 23). Authority creates this safety. In a household where true authority exists, it is safe to take bold steps of faith. It is safe to share your weaknesses and struggles. It is safe to grapple with the things you do not understand. It is safe to confess unbelief. It is safe to prioritise relationship with Christ over exam results.

Authority kicks the enemy out of our households. There is a great scene in the film War Room where the lead character, a mother, whose family has been falling apart, takes up her authority and literally opens the front door of her house and commands the enemy to leave, and then slams it shut, no longer giving him room. That is creating the safety of the Kingdom. A place where things like living for financial gain and academic achievement, as well as the evils of pornography and other addictions are not exerting their influence on our family at home.

Another aspect of God's Kingdom we express in the home is learning obedience. Safety makes it attractive to be obedient. Our job as parents is to teach our children obedience, a word very much out of fashion yet so vital if they are to walk with Jesus. *'If you love me you will keep my commandments' (John 14:15).*

Children should do what their parents ask them to. The challenge always starts with us, so am I coming from a place of submission to the throne of God, where all my actions are directed towards glorifying Christ? Where, as we talked about earlier, authority is not like the world's lording it over our children, barking out orders, or demanding they toe the line. Obedience should be talked about. The classic child's question 'why must I do this?' met with 'because I say so!' isn't generally good enough. If we have Kingdom authority, then we can explain why and be humble enough to realise sometimes we demand things that have no real justification. We create a safe, humble authority that can be obeyed straight away when needed - like the child running toward a busy road - but also one where we go beyond the letter of the law, to the heart.

We need to prepare our children to obey God. If they are to walk with God, they will have to make choices to obey or not. I read recently about an Iranian lady who was at her father's funeral when an older man arrived, who had consistently sexually abused her over a number of years. She was afraid, but God said to her 'I have brought him here so you can forgive him.' She knew how to obey. She understood submission and so forgave him, despite the pain. She said, 'Instantly, as I forgave this man, my heart was healed, and I was completely set free from all those years of abuse!' God didn't negotiate with her. He didn't dangle a carrot or manipulate. He just asked her to do something, and she did it, and it changed her life.

I obey God because I trust and love him.

True authority enables our children to grow up knowing the joy and freedom of obedience. If you are safe, then it's more likely they will know that God is safe.

Authority comes to the fore when things are difficult, or there is a difference of opinion. We have been through a season of late where our daughter has struggled with being home-schooled. She felt she was missing out, and that valuable experiences were being lost. At times she felt alienated from her friends and was finding this really hard.

When you are doing something sacrificial, (home-schooling costs us), and something you believe is right, true authority sets you free to engage with those involved in humility and sensitivity. It's rooted in identity, so, whereas her unhappiness could have been perceived as a threat to our choices, or a lack of submission to our vision, instead we treated it with respect.

We talked with her. Listened to her and then spent considerable time talking, chewing over and praying through our decision. Authority sets you free from having to be right, but it also enables you to make tough choices well. No-one wants their children to be unhappy, and we genuinely grappled with the question whether our choices were harming her. However, after going round and round on at least a dozen occasions, we felt we were doing the right thing, had faith it would work out and also the freedom to make the call.

We sat together, talked, and all shed a few tears. She knew we felt her pain, sense of loneliness and loss. We heard her heart and gently shared our decision to continue home-schooling and why we felt we should. We encouraged her to give it to Jesus, trusting that even if mum and dad were wrong, God would still work it out for her good.

And we prayed. Happily, she is currently content and making the most of the time she is in. Leadership is not fundamentally about making decisions, but when they do come, authority helps us do it well.

On mission

And finally, this safety that authority creates, enables those within that household or church family to begin to express that Kingdom authority in their own lives. I experienced this first-hand when I was part of someone else's 'household' in Mozambique.

> 'Everyone who has their hand in the air has a back problem and needs healing. Go!'

The moonlight was forgivingly strong that night as there were no streetlights or for that matter electricity out there in 'proper' Africa, so I could make out at least 100 hands held aloft each confessing a need and a hope. Anthony (tall Aussie friend) and I pushed into the crowd of maybe 1500 and one of the most amazing moments of my life unfurled like a pristine sail. We were somewhere in the 'bush bush', as Iris Global likes to term it. Three deaf children had just been healed, (one deaf and dumb from birth), as Heidi Baker had called for them to be brought forward, and Iris Children (formerly orphans) aged maybe 10-12, had prayed.

Anthony and I stood in the middle of the crowd for maybe 45 minutes, and every single person we prayed for was healed. Now normally I am quite happy if the people I pray for don't get worse, so this was not my normal gig. We had person after person humbly approach us, point to their back problem (lower, middle, upper, whole thing, neck, hip etc.) utter a few words in Makhuwa (local dialect), which we didn't understand, as they tried to bend. They would then look at us with kind, expectant eyes. I must confess that the first time I prayed I was trying to figure out how to communicate that God still loved them even if they weren't healed, when the old man suddenly began touching his toes with a big smile on his face. After that we just went with it, simply, gently, blessing the person and asking Jesus to heal them. And He did!!

It was crazy. At one point we had some demonically possessed individuals come over and try to disrupt us, by uttering chants and releasing evil unearthly cackles. Unfortunately for them, the presence of the Holy Spirit was so strong that these attempts were met with joy and peace overflowing on our part, and every person still kept getting healed. We had man after man come to us cap in hand (sign of respect), repenting and wanting to get free from alcohol addiction. It was humbling and wonderful to see each one receive a touch of grace from Jesus.

Nothing like this had ever happened in my life. It was beyond anything I have yet to personally walk in, and although this is an extreme example, it illustrates that the more authority you walk in, the more you enable those around you to experience and walk in the benefits of the Kingdom. I think that is the dream God has about you being a spiritual parent and a leader; about your family. About you being a disciple, about your church.

Authority is the revelation of your identity in Christ, and from this, the laying down of your life in the service of others.

Seeing everyone getting healed is gospel crazy. This was my experience of just how good God is and how I really had never grasped how good He could be through me.

The joy of authority is how it unlocks the kingdom value of extravagance. Read on.

Reflection on Authority

By Kathryn

The weekend I left my family in Mozambique proved to be a turning point in authority for me, my journey of knowing my identity in Christ and laying that down to serve others.

Now Matt was perfectly capable of looking after our three kids (then ages 9, 7, 5) for two days on the Iris base we had gotten used to over the last two months, it turned out to be more about the faith journey I was on. I had been getting to spend lots of time in God's presence, having amazingly inspirational, passionate teaching and finding out who I really was. I was discovering my identity and what He had called me to. Ethan and I had done one weekend outreach into the African bush and I felt overall very stretched as we neared the end of our Harvest School experience.

Then the leaders shared that there was one more weekend outreach coming up in the second to last week of our whole training. There were spaces on that trip. I thought 'Oh Matt should do that, it would be great for him!' Matt said to me 'You should go on that!' Inwardly I resisted and felt like all I wanted to do was start organising and preparing myself ready to go home to England. The more I felt like I didn't want to go, the more I actually felt that it was something I should do. Any mum-like argument I came up with about kids needing me here was washed away by God's Spirit gently prompting me that surely the best thing I could do for my kids was show them that my faith looked like something, it was adventure. Deep down I knew that in the long run putting my faith-journey with Him above my kids was going to bear fruit!

So I went. Crammed into the back of a jeep with a bunch of Americans (who were on a two-week mission trip to

Mozambique), bags, tents and Mozambican pastors, we travelled on bumpy roads for several hours. After pitching our little tents in a sandy compound in a random village, we put up a huge screen and showed the Jesus movie to the villagers. The next morning we split into small groups with the aim to walk round the village handing out Bibles. That morning my little team did not get more than 200 yards from our tent base as person after person came up to us asking for a Bible and wanting us to lead them to Jesus! We really did next to nothing. It was incredible! About 20 people. At one point, well into this experience, as we were praying for someone, I took a step back incredulous at what God was doing. He literally dropped into my spirit the words 'This is what I wanted to show you Kathryn. **I AM**. The way I am drawing people to myself here, I will do in England too.'

This alone was amazing, but it blew me away even more because my questions to God before coming to Mozambique, had been 'Why are we going there? Why do I need to go there?' His reply had been 'Because I want to show you what I am doing!' I had assumed He wanted me to see blind eyes opening, deaf ears hearing and lame walking. But no, more than that He wanted to change my heart and understanding of salvation. That moment and the rest of the weekend was so profound, that whilst of course I missed my family and you couldn't see my feet for dirt by the end of it, something in that wild, free weekend enabled me to really understand who God was and what He was calling me to be.

I used to hate evangelism and find it embarrassing but that weekend I grew in authority as a disciple of Jesus by simply going with Him and watching Him work. It's hard to put into words really but it was a big part of my journey in giving me 100% more confidence in showing my children Jesus and leading others to Him. If I hadn't said yes to going on that small adventure with Jesus, then the many in England who have come to know Him since we came to Highworth would still be lost. Through my role at our local Christians Against Poverty (CAP) centre and wider as part of CAP's evangelism team, I have had the confidence as a daughter of the King to share the most precious and good news with many people!

If you are a mum and you feel a God-prompt to step out in faith but your nesting, protective instincts seem to over-ride, I want to encourage you...go for it!

Four

Extravagance

*'But while he was still a long way off, his father saw him and was
filled with compassion for him; he ran to his son, threw his arms
around him and kissed him.'*

Luke 15:20

My foggy, just woken up mind was pierced by a scream and a
crash. My wife's scream. Every nerve cell jumped to life and
a thousand thoughts bolted through my mind as I raced from
the bedroom to the far end of our flat to see our car backed
through a wall.

Kathryn had been helping one of our children with their paper
round, because they had a cold, by taking them round in the
car. Unfortunately, being a little tired and a little rushed she
had forgotten to apply the handbrake and jumped out of the
car, only for gravity and the gentle slope of our driveway to
slowly but unrelentingly propel the car backwards and
through our neighbour's wall! Fortunately everyone was
alright but our new car was not.

This was our prophetic car.

Way back at a rather good church meeting in 2008 I received a
prophetic word : 'I see you driving around England in a bus
or a van full of people. Every town or village that you visit I
see you all getting out and preaching the gospel.'

I had never thought of doing this. It was not a vision I had and I didn't really want to be a travelling evangelist but I believed it. The Holy Spirit in me witnessed to this word instantly and I knew it was God. I wrote it down, prayed and trusted that God would reveal more in the right time.

Fast forward eight years and I was way more up for evangelism, and freshly stirred to reach out with the good news to other places, but we were car-less. I was reminded of that word, what if now is the time? We can't go unless we have something to go in, so why not buy a big car?

The more we prayed about this as a family the more convinced we became and our faith grew. As usual we didn't have a lot of money but undeterred I searched Google to discover what would be the best vehicle. We needed something that would double as a 'normal' car, as well as a travelling revival bus, and my research pointed to the VW Caravelle. It could hold seven adults in proper seats really comfortably and still leave room for luggage, whilst being remarkably compact and a great drive. Perfect. They're just really expensive. So we prayed more and felt to step out and at least look at one.

A couple of days later Steve Lee, a great friend and gifted evangelist, was visiting to share with our church. I had popped out for a walk and as I neared home a thought flashed in my mind, 'Steve Lee has bought a VW Caravelle.' As I turned the corner there was Steve sitting in a lovely, new to him, metallic grey Caravelle. OK... Not only that but found out God had miraculously provided for Steve – was this the confirmation we needed?

So we prayed, believed God would provide and went for it. I can remember the next couple of weeks, after purchasing the car with a loan, checking the mailbox daily, convinced the money would arrive. It didn't... and then the crash.

I don't know if you have ever hit your thumb with a hammer. Once is painful but when you do it a second time the pain is off the charts. So five months later I was lying in bed contemplating the coming day and my reflections were pierced with another scream from Kathryn and the déjà vu sound of my car backing through the same wall. My heart sank like a brick.

The first time it happened I was full of grace and trust, this time I felt sucked under a sea of 'why God?' and some other choice thoughts about my wife. The money hadn't appeared to pay off the loan and now, two insurance claims later, we were very much up against it. We went back to God, checked our hearts, worshipped and prayed into the place of trust and just held on.

Over the next two and a half years we had moments where it all made sense. Team trips in the van were fantastic. You could pray and worship together all the way and all the way back and we started to see the prophetic word fulfilled. We even received a crazy confirmation word. A man came up to me from one of the teams when we visited Bethel Church in California and said 'I don't know if this means anything but I see you driving a bus full of Christians around the UK and stopping in towns and villages to share the gospel.' That was quite encouraging!

Despite these rays of light it was still hard, and during that whole time we kept praying, kept grappling and God kept saying 'keep going.' However the opportunities and energy to travel were not in proportion to the amount of money it was still costing us and we really struggled as to whether it was worth it. On top of that Ethan was now old enough to learn to drive and we needed something smaller for him, so in the summer of 2019 we decided to sell the car. We reasoned we could always buy another one down the road and that maybe we had just got the timing wrong. Fortunately Caravelles are one of the few vehicles that hold their value so it looked like we could sell, pay off the remaining loan and buy a decent smaller family car.

I felt really good, like a weight had been lifted, as I took some photos and uploaded my sale on to Auto Trader. Hitting your thumb twice hurts. Smacking yourself round the head is agony.

The first interested buyer questioned some inconsistencies with the mileage we quoted, compared with what was recorded on the gov.uk MOT website. On investigation it looked like our car had been clocked, we had been taken advantage of and the real mileage was around 130000 miles more! Arrggh. This meant the car would be worth half of what we trying to sell it for.

For the last few months we have tried to get to the bottom of what's happened and it is still inconclusive. There is little we can do but pray, wait and keep searching and so due to this we are stuck with the car for now.

I've titled this chapter 'Extravagance.' Why on earth would I start a chapter about the abundance and goodness of God with this story? Surely this deserves to go in a 'life sucks but we keep going' chapter? I've started here for a reason but allow me to lay some groundwork first.

There is always enough

I have chosen to use the word extravagance to describe a lifestyle of living with a God who is good, and will be good to you and to me, because it has yet to be 'Christianised'. You know, when a word is so often used it loses its power and becomes some objective truth we know we should agree with yet fail to experience in our here and now.

Our God is an extravagant God and don't just take my word for it. The Apostle Paul knew a thing or two about God and he kicks off his letter to his friends in Ephesus with an extravagant declaration:

'Praise be to the God and Father of our Lord Jesus Christ, who has blessed us in the heavenly realms with every spiritual blessing in Christ.' (Ephesians 1:3)

And then. He loses it, and the wonder of it all overtakes him and without pause (no commas or full stops in the whole passage - my kind of grammar) he unleashes a wondrous revelation of this thing we call Christianity. It is crammed full of exotic and enticing words: Blessed. Every. Chosen. Holy. Blameless. Love. Pre-destined ('great destiny'). Adopted, Pleasure. Glorious Grace. Freely. Redemption. Forgiveness. Riches. Lavished. And that is just from five verses! This is Paul writing his, and every other Christ follower's, Curriculum Vitae. Reading it makes me feel like the most adored, centre-of-attention, valued child, of the richest, most powerful and utterly safe Father anyone could ever have.

Paul is saying God is extravagant and so is the salvation He gives us.

When I hear that word extravagant, it conjures images of opulent cribs in Beverly Hills or some pop star draped in bling. Worldly extravagance is gluttonous indulgence. But even a godly extravagance is not a word many Christians would use to describe their faith, and yet: *'He has rescued us from the dominion of darkness and brought us into the kingdom of the Son he loves,' (Colossians 1:17).*

And for free!

Maybe no story better illustrates the extravagance of God than the one with the little lad and his packed lunch in John chapter 6:1-14.

Here's a vast number of normal people (we know there were 5,000 men, so could have been a crowd of 10,000 plus), people whose lives were probably hard, poor, repetitive and filled with responsibility. People who had bags of common sense and very down to earth expectations.

So rather against the grain, they all find themselves in the middle of nowhere, having no food and no plan B. They have followed the pied piper of Nazareth, with His miracles and words, into the wilderness, where there was now serious danger of mass fainting, hospitalisation and even death. What were they thinking?

Their hunger for Jesus had drawn them to a place where only the extravagance of God would sustain their lives.

Jesus takes this little lunch, breaks the loaves and fish in thankfulness (which shows us how closely connected being thankful and faith are), and then as the pieces are handed out, an incredible multiplication happens. Everyone has something to eat and not just a conservative portion, but everyone was satisfied; you know that full, 'I probably shouldn't have had that extra roast potato,' feeling!

But the miracle doesn't even stop there, twelve basketfuls (full baskets) of leftover bread and fish were collected up by the disciples.

Wow and well... what? Why the extras? Surely, God is clever enough to provide exactly the right amount of food for each person? Or even a slightly liberal amount, in case someone was a little greedy, or to account for floor droppage. Some genius maths angel could have divided the number of people by calorie requirements, and a food multiplication algorithm could have been created for that and future food related miracles. Why too much?

This is a window into the character of our God. He is not some divine housewife, frugally eking out salvation, or a workman labouring with limited resources. Simply, this miracle of thousands of full tummies, and a huge pile of leftovers screams: 'There is always enough! God is extravagant!'

This Kingdom extravagance is in direct conflict with the world system. Out there you have what you have. To get more you have to work for it. You can't do anything you don't have the resources to do. To survive you have to divide your resources, apportioning what you have to different obligations and needs. To achieve more, you have to borrow, and you pay back more than you were lent. The world's system is one of limitation, ceilings and constraints.

And we have bought into it.

Now you can live in the world system well or badly, depending upon your choices. Too many credit cards, loans and living beyond your means and the system fails you. Act shrewdly, diligently managing what you have, limiting your choices to your socioeconomic class, add a good dose of common sense and luck and you can generally survive. To be 'successful' in this world takes a good stewarding of resources and whilst my above focus is finance, it includes time, health, relationships and your possessions.

Sadly, this 'stewardship' has become the adopted western Christian's modus operandi. A wise working of a system that is not God's.

The stewardship error

Let's look at a famous parable, one I believe typifies our complete misunderstanding of how we think God wants us to live. The parable of the Talents or Three Servants found in Matthew chapter 25:14-30.

Jesus told parables to reveal something - to make a point. The key is understanding the point and responding to it. Like any passage of scripture, we need to first look at what it meant to the people who originally heard it, and secondly what it means to us here and now, several centuries later. And that is rather simple.

Three servants are given differing amounts of money (talents) and judged on what they did with it. Did they put it to work? Did they increase the original investment? The point to the original hearers and to us, is that God (the master) has given and is giving us (the servants) something that we are supposed to put to work, and in so doing bring an increase in the original investment. We are supposed to be good stewards.

So what have we been given that we will be held to account for? How <u>do</u> we put it to work?

What about the literal translation? The original Hebrew word actually means money. A talent was a measure of money. Is Jesus saying that you must steward your money well, that my life is judged on what I do with my finances? Some people are given small, medium and large amounts of money in life - ok we can see that. But, taking this to the literal conclusion, are we as good followers of Christ supposed to make more money from what we have been given, and find that the most celebrated people in eternity are those who had lots of money to start with and then made huge amounts more? That is not the gospel, that's the 'American Dream'. Jesus celebrated giving away, not accumulating more!

So, a big fat NO to that one.

This parable was a favourite in Sunday School when I was growing up and probably still is today. Sunday school teachers love the fact that for us, using the English language, the word talent is not a unit of money but your skills and abilities. We would all sit discussing our talents - what we were good at and the 'gifts' God had given us. Lovely. So the teaching becomes, if you play the guitar, play well, if you bake, bake well, if you can run, then fun fast, if you are good at French then *'bien parler'* .. It's nice for kids but has nothing to do with what Jesus was trying to teach. Really, do you anticipate your heavenly inheritance to be based on your achievements with whatever skills you had? Here I am Lord, and here is my 50m swimming badge! Again, we end up with an elitist gospel, the most talented among us will be given the most. Is Jesus really going to be upset about my neglected bike riding skills?

Making use of your particular talents to glorify God is great, but not what this parable is about.

So what is it?

I like Todd White's definition. For me, it fits like your favourite pair of well-worn jeans (which is utterly perfectly, if you don't have some). It's about Grace. Grace is what we are given and are supposed to put to work. Irrespective of financial ability and physical and mental capability, every follower of Christ has experienced and received Grace.

Ephesians chapter 4:7 says, *'But to each one of us grace has been given as Christ apportioned it.'*

Yes, grace is given without measure, but I recognise that in this moment right now there is a measure of grace that I have been blessed to know and experience. I have the same Saviour as Peter but have yet to walk in his experience of grace! I long to walk in more, seek after the faith to access more, but am called to live up to the measure I have been given, by investing my experience, my grace, in others. Grace is an unmerited blessing, and we give this to others through our time, energy, love, compassion, financial giving, encouragement and sharing of the truth. Stewardship of this commodity is all about increase! The focus is more. God's grace is life and it multiplies in everyone it encounters. The grace that has touched me, I put to use to touch countless others!

Sadly, stewardship has become a wonderful endorsement for risk averse, limited, cautious, self-preserving and boring Christianity. It looks and feels 'Christian', sensible and responsible, yet makes no sense and creates unresponsive Christians. Does leaving your nets and following Jesus look like stewardship in our view?

A good steward

There was a man called John G Lake who is one of my heroes. He's the guy who started and ran the Healing Rooms in Spokane, Washington back in 1915, where for five years up to 200 people a day were ministered to, most being unchurched, and most being healed. For that period, according to government statistics, Spokane was the healthiest city in the world!

Anyhow, years before that, Mr Lake was a successful businessman earning, according to my little research with an inflation calculator, over $3 million. At the same time, he was ministering in divine healing and the gifts of the Holy Spirit. He was a man about God's business, and a man of wealth. Then God called him and his family to Africa.

So here he is sitting on a fortune, surely you make some investments, set up a trust or start a charity to support your call. You would at least use the money 'wisely' to book tickets and provide for your family. Nope, he and his wife Jennie give away or sell everything they own, believing God has called them to be entirely dependent upon him. They then have to spend considerable time in prayer for the needed mission finances, and, it then gets even crazier, they end up queuing (a line for our US friends) for the steamer to take to South Africa, without the money to even buy the tickets and secure their entry. How irresponsible!?

Between 1908 and 1912 Lake saw over 100,000 people give their lives to Jesus and planted 625 churches in southern Africa.

That's stewardship!

So, what if it's really that simple and that scary? We just keep giving and He provides. In the Kingdom of God, extravagance is a foundational belief that God will provide as I live by faith, responding 'yes' to everything He calls me to do.

The context of this talent's parable on 'stewardship' sheds even more light on this revelation. Jesus has just had His famous encounter with a supposedly vertically challenged guy called Zacchaeus. Here's a man who exemplifies the 'good and faithful servant'. He receives grace as God stops for him, sees him and despite opposition, stays in his home. Immediately this grace, this extravagance, produces something, and in one of the most incredible responses to a Jesus encounter on record, Zacchaeus parts with over half his wealth, without even being asked.

Grace is predisposed to reproduce.

Sunburn and grace

One of Iris Global's values is 'There is always enough,' which is another way of saying 'God is extravagant,' or 'God is good'. I experienced this first-hand one morning in Mozambique. The day before, like any good Brit, I had got sunburnt during a walk on the beach. That evening, to relieve the minor pain and soreness, my wife kindly applied Aloe Vera to the parched skin but instead of that refreshing cooling experience, all I got was pain. In seconds, like some extreme acupuncture, my entire back came alive as if a thousand needles were being drilled into it. Despite a couple of showers, this less than pleasant experience lasted the entire night, through which I spent most of the time clenching my fists, biting my lip and trying not to cry out in pain and wake the house (what a hero)!

In the morning the pain began to subside, but Kathryn fetched Annelie (the Iris staff nurse) who quickly explained the problem. Being good parents, we had forked out for the expensive Malarone anti-malarial for our children, and again like good parents had gone for the cheaper doxycycline for ourselves. One of the side effects to doxy is photosensitivity, and the combination of burnt skin and aloe vera had sent my skin cells into an extreme overreaction.

'You need to stop taking doxycycline,' Annelie stated.

Okay. Agreed. But what do I do instead? Malaria was a serious risk, and my brain went into overdrive trying to figure out how and where I could secure some Malarone.

Quick history lesson. Mozambique suffered a horrific civil war between 1977 and 1992, which destroyed most of its infrastructure and industrial production. Nearly 20 years later it was still reeling in the aftermath and most products, other than local grown foods, had to be shipped in from other countries. This meant, for example, a big mango cost about ten pence and a jar of peanut butter £5. In my head, the only option was getting the medication airlifted in from South Africa, which would take time and a lot of money.

'I'll pop and see if we have any in our store,' Annelie volunteered. 'Past students often donate leftover medication and there's a chance we have some.' A ray of hope pierced the dense clouds of my swirling thoughts. She returned ten minutes later and matter-of-factly handed over a handful of

Malarone boxes. 'Here you go, that's all we have and it's exactly enough to see you through the next seven weeks.'

And it hit me (I may have actually cried). Here she was handing me at least £250 of medication for free, at a mission base that was always financially challenged, with no thought of holding anything back. This was all they had!

There was no rationing of resources. We in our western mind-set would have held some back for a 'rainy day,' assigned me just enough until we could order some more. Not here. I could see it on Annelie's face, this faith, this belief that Jesus has us, there is always enough, that our job is to meet every need extravagantly with whatever we have, trusting that the next need Jesus will provide for. Here was a need and praise God we can meet it.

Oh, the beautiful, courageous simplicity.

Extravagance is about living with a God upon whom you trust for everything. You live utterly free from the need to store up for yourself or wrap your identity in the accumulation of more and more things, which is the world's extravagance where it is about you, about being selfish. A Kingdom extravagance is about Jesus - it's self-less. That's the simple difference.

Extravagance in action.

The prosperity gospel says God will give you a healthy body, money in the bank, a new car, a thriving family and boundless happiness. It's a worldly twisting of the truth of a lavish God that centres on me, rather than on the Kingdom. Extravagance is a heart condition, not a bank balance! It sets you free to live undefined by your circumstances because you know God has you, that He can meet any need, that He will provide, and you can then be . . . content! You can be poor or rich and still live extravagantly and still live content.

We have a terrible kitchen in our rented flat. It is at least 35 years old. A couple of drawers don't open properly, funny black dusty stuff coats anything left in one of the cupboards for any length of time, and it's magnolia. I built a dream kitchen in our previous home years ago. We extended our house to accommodate it, everything was carefully chosen, beautiful wooden worktops, specially designed splashback, stainless steel tiles, heated wooden floor and a baby blue SMEG classic fridge. It was gorgeous. Strange thing is, I am way more content with the crappy one I cook in now, than the expensive one from back then. Why? Because I am learning an amazing secret.

'I have learned to be content whatever the circumstances. I know what it is to be in need, and I know what it is to have plenty. I have learned the secret of being content in any and every situation, whether well fed or hungry, whether living in plenty or in want. I can do all this through him who gives me strength.' (Philippians 4:11-13)

Someone sharing a secret with you is always a special moment, and here Paul shares a beauty. You can be content whatever your circumstances! Phone the BBC, get a plane to write the words in the sky, send up a flare, someone post this on Twitter! You and I can be utterly content, every single day, whatever happens, content even when we are without, because contentment does not flow from possessing what you need and more, it comes from and through Jesus.

Contentment flows from Jesus not from stuff.

This is something we are discovering and paradoxically has been a fruit of extravagance. You see extravagance is all about living free. I can receive extravagantly, and I can give extravagantly. Contentment puts my focus onto the provision of God, not the possibilities defined by my own resources.

Here's a little example from September 2012, the day we moved into our first rented home since selling our house and most of our stuff mid-2011. I had meant to go and buy a washing machine, but time ran away with me, and I realised at 7.55pm that evening that I couldn't get to the shops in time. The phone rang five minutes later and a lady called Brenda, I hardly knew at the time from our new church said, 'we are just clearing out my Dad's place and there is a washing machine that he no longer needs - would you like it?'

What if God really knows our needs, plans for their provision in His timing and what if it's better than what you would have done?

The next day I had a phone call from someone I don't think I'd even properly met, (guy called Clive), asking if we would like a chest of drawers. 'Yes please.' I shot round in the car. It was a really solid piece of furniture and in good condition. Thank you, God. 'Do you need anything else?' Clive asked. I thought about it, and on the off chance enquired if he knew someone who had a double bed frame, as we were sleeping on a mattress on the floor. Clive scratched his head and then headed off into his garage. He returned with a polythene wrapped, brand new, solid oak double bed frame. 'I have this one, if you would like it?'

This secret hit me. I was free. I had gladly sold and given stuff away, to my financial loss, and now I was happy, just resting in the detailed, knowing, provision of God. I was happy giving and happy receiving. I was living with 'there is always enough' and I was content.

I have visited the jungle temples of Angkor Wat, walked on the golden sands of Langkawi, been on several African safaris, eaten in posh restaurants and driven a Bentley Continental. Extravagance means I can enjoy 'riches' without it entering my heart or demanding it become my norm. Extravagance is a heart condition. An expectation of provision and a trust filled rest in the waiting.

It enables us to give and to receive, and it is something we have discovered and lived in more and more as a family.

Lessons in Extravagance

Extravagance, like many of the things in this book, informs our culture. It affects everything, how we speak, think, spend, act and prioritise. As we have attempted to live this out, we've been fascinated to see several positive side effects. These, of course, are not the reason we pursue extravagance and do not happen in isolation, as this isn't some Christian family maths formulae! However, here are four effects an extravagant culture has had on our family:

1. Service.

Our children do not do chores. They do not have a list of jobs they need to do every week or have to keep their room to an expected level of cleanliness. This was purposeful. They happily join in when things need doing, do not generally need even to be asked to wash-up after dinner because from an early age we involved them in our lives. Our home is their home, and we all take responsibility for its upkeep. To do this we have been willing to change our expectations as parents. We are not demanding they do things in the exact and perfect way that we might like, but try to organically find how we want to run our home together. Extravagance does this because it stops us from doing life from a 'mine viewpoint'. It's not my money or my time. Putting out the bins is not robbing them of their Xbox time, it's just a part of life. And this should be a joyful service. Kathryn and I love serving, and I really struggle with reluctant, miserable servers. I put chairs out at church gladly because I am doing it for Jesus, and we have gone out of our way to teach our children the same, not to think of any job too low, or to try and get away with doing as little as possible. We serve together, everywhere, all the time. Service is the best way of involving them in the Kingdom because that is the Kingdom - if the King *'didn't come to be served but to serve,'* then we shall do the same (Mark 10:28). Recently one of my children discovered something unmentionable smeared on one of the toilet doors when we were setting up for Sunday Church at the school we hire. They followed this up with 'Do you want me to clean it off?'

2. Atmosphere.

We don't do stress because God is good and He will be good to us. There is a startling lack of arguments in our home. Challenges still come at us and we often find ourselves in stressful times, but we intentionally choose to reject our reactions and instead believe there is always enough energy, time, money and grace. We joke, have fun, talk openly and honestly and do life. We don't shout at our children and they don't shout at each other or us. We actively reject stress and extravagance has helped us remove 'clash' points. For example, if keeping your home ultra-tidy and having to cajole or force your children to fulfil that ideal causes battles and negativity, is it worth it? As I have shared in this book, control so easily can dominate our lives and consequently the upkeep of my home can end up being an expression of this control rather than love! I appreciate for many of you this might sound radical or even ridiculous. Extravagance, which means there is always enough, has enabled us to be happy with some mess, happy when we leave things until tomorrow and made life more enjoyable, peaceful and fun!

3. Generosity.

I remember a little lad we were working with in Cambodia, who was new to the Dream Centre project for street children. When it came to toy time piles of dinky cars, Lego and action figures were poured out onto the reed mats, he quickly gathered as much as he could into his lap, and desperately spent the next thirty minutes trying to hang on to them, rather than play. That's what we call an orphan spirit. Extravagance enables us to play, to enjoy, rather than fight and store. This is why we haven't ever given our children pocket money. Teaching them extravagance was more important than good money management. We intentionally wanted them to learn to trust, rather than possess, to enjoy us providing for them, and to be content when this looked like less, rather than more. We are supposed to show them the Father, and that is exactly how He wants us to live. Interestingly, as they have now all got part-time jobs and a healthy income, they act responsibly with their finances and are generous. Our kids are always happy to give and are far better at it than me! They see 'their' money less as 'theirs'. It's just money and can be freely used for a whole host of things.

4. **You can say 'no!'**

Extravagance creates contentment, which enables your children to be happy when you say no. This is big. We currently have teenagers, and they are supposed to be in their 'pushing the boundaries' years. A 'no' should be met with stomped feet, deep groans, slouched shoulders and a general exasperated frustration at how unfair life is. 'You don't understand!' Instead, our attempts to live in God's extravagance is creating in them a freeing trust. Trust is crucial because it enables them to believe that a 'no' can actually be the best answer.

Back to the prophetic car

I love the picture of our Father that Jesus paints in His parable of the Lost Son (Luke chapter 15:11-31). The Father's arms-open-wide acceptance of His son merits on the scandalous. The son who rejected his father and wasted all his money is welcomed lavishly home. This is the challenge of extravagance, to know God for who He really is and live like Him.

'God is good all the time. And all the time, God is good.' So often this statement is a cheesy expression of a reality we can rarely see or we rarely know. Experiences like we have had with our car (and far worse) dominate many of our existences upon this planet. And so whilst we may declare God is good, we struggle to believe that He will be good to me.

King David finishes one of my favourite Psalms with the confident proclamation that: *'I will see the goodness of God in the land of the living,'* (Psalm 27:13). Saying God is good is one thing, confidently believing He will be good to me is another.

I wanted to start this chapter with the drama of our 'prophetic car' story because this deeper magic of extravagance has meant the difference between it being an ongoing nightmare, and instead an ongoing experience of a good God. It is within this stuff, the doubt and the grey, the silence and the struggle that we see and know the real, Father-open-wide-arms-running-toward-me God.

- It's ok when things go wrong because God is good
- It's ok when things don't work out because God is good
- It's ok when I am ripped off because God is good
- It's ok when I question my actions because God is good

Did I make perfect decisions? I don't think so. Did I have faith at all times? Definitely not. Did I beat myself up and blame my lack of understanding? Yes. Is God good through all of this? Absolutely.

Extravagance is the interweaving of the goodness of God in the complexities of our life. It is not everything being sorted, needs met immediately, everything fine. It is something far better, far deeper, far more wonderful. It flows from a freedom, gladly submitted to God, that rests in the twists and the turns of life, solid on the foundation that He is good, will be good and nothing can stop Him being good. Nothing can resist his goodness. Even when I fail and I am frail, when I miss it and I struggle, His goodness is running after me.

Today I don't have a clue what the end of the car story will be and do you know what? It doesn't matter, because:

Extravagance is the conviction that God is good and He will be good to you.

The challenge with this extravagance - with this freedom to live with much or little, unwavering in your belief and expectation that God is good and will be good, demands a brutal level of reality. I want to be honest with you in the next chapter. Read on.

Reflection on Extravagance

By Ethan

Now I have never been exiled, stoned or ship-wrecked but there has been a lot of movement over the 18 years of my life. I have lived in 10 different places spread out across three continents and visited many more countries. Our family of five have lived in a 260 m², seven-bedroom, five bathroom, three conservatory house and also in nine m² of cold, bare concrete with not even a toilet to call our own! Yet within this menagerie of experiences I can say that I cannot think of a place that I would remember negatively. 'Not negative' is however a far cry from the complete contentment that Paul claims. I certainly still have a way to go.

When I woke up in Cambodia to discover for the tenth day running that the world's stealthiest mosquitos had penetrated two doors, multiple sprays, pyjamas, socks and skin to deliver three painfully irritating bites, I can't say that I was very content! When I discovered that in yet another home I am still going to have to share a room with my brother, still not having a space that I can fully control or that is totally mine, I wasn't incredibly content.

However despite the hiccups and the trials I can honestly say that there is not one of the ten homes we have lived in that I disliked or didn't enjoy.

At every point, God has always been good whether through an abundant Thanksgiving feast breaking up a dull monotony of rice and beans, a snorkelling trip in Cambodia when we started to feel homesick, cheap restaurants to eat delicious food after working in the slums or getting to enjoy the freedoms of home school after a few years of bullying.

For me, experiencing the extravagance of God has been less about the big things and more about his goodness in the hard days. One of my hardest days was when I was 14 and we were travelling with some friends to visit ATE (a charity they were connected with) in Ghana. In order to reach ATE's base of operations we had to take an armed escort bus from the capital Accra in the south, to the small town of Lawra at the very north of the country. This was supposed to be a 15 hour journey through the night, keyword 'supposed'. By the end we had been travelling for 22 hours! Almost everything that could go wrong did go wrong, from the AC unit breaking down and delaying our departure by 2 hours to some form of engine failure before we even made it out of the city. From there we managed a couple of hours of travel before undeveloped African roads made their presence known. The bumpy ride was accentuated by the inescapable, spiritually disturbing soap operas about murderers and witch doctors blaring through the TV screen right in front of our seats.

However as we prayed during the journey, God showed his goodness! The disturbing soap opera was turned off and the radio started playing Hillsong worship music! (Where did that come from?) Yet despite all this trouble, despite the heat and exhaustion, I can say I never felt stressed or anxious during the journey. I had a distinct feeling of God's presence and peace throughout the entire bus drive. Whether through a bout of Hillsong worship or a surprisingly deep sleep, God showed and has continued to show His extravagance, proving that I do not need to worry myself, I can trust and therefore be content.

Five

Honesty

'But if we walk in the light, as he is in the light, we have fellowship with one another, and the blood of Jesus, his Son, purifies us from all sin.'

1 John 1:7

'Daddy I am worried. What if God doesn't supply?'

It was January 2018 and I was putting my then 11-year-old daughter to bed when she, full of real concern, shared her deepest fear. We had been seeking God as a family about a mission trip to the US and taken the plunge, we booked flights. We didn't have the money, had no foreseeable way of getting the money and we had shared this openly with the children. Five thousand pounds on a hope and a prayer.

And here she was grappling with that great question, the one all of us Christ followers cannot escape. Does God provide? More importantly, will he provide for me? Yes, surely God provides when we are in dire straits with no means and no way out, but does he provide for easily avoided Atlantic crossings that are based less on need and more on a gut feeling?

What do you say? What do you say to a young life that is questioning whether mummy and daddy can save the day and if not, will this belief in, and life with, an invisible God really work?

I was tired and could have easily palmed her off with a false, confident 'I am sure it will all be ok,' or the slightly better 'God will provide for all our needs' (like quoting scripture answers everything). Instead I paused and honoured her honesty with mine.

'I know what you mean. I am worried as well.' And I really was.

So instead of trying to make her feel better, we prayed to the only one who held the answer and cast our burdens upon Him.

I learned this, a counter-cultural sharing as a family in the good and the challenging, from Clive, a slightly gangly, proper Englishman with an insatiable appetite for God, and from his wife Beth, a woman of rare faith.

I have precious memories of going out for lunch with Clive, normally a Chinese meal, and just hearing his heart, his struggles and hopes. I was a naive, idealistic young man of twenty, working under Clive at Immanuel Church in Winchester as a Youth Pastor and he was exactly what I needed. Yes, he believed in miracles, but he believed in hard work, in giving your life, in sacrificing as well. Although a church pastor, his full-time job was as a director of an architect firm, which on its own would probably cause most people a nervous breakdown! The combination gave him a unique perspective, and he was slightly critical of how he perceived many in 'full-time' ministry. Under his tutelage I developed an improved work ethic (I previously had tended to work in fits and starts), which I hope I still walk out today. His no-nonsense approach was brilliant. I remember walking up Winchester High Street and asking him if I should ask Kathryn to marry me. I was laying it out before him, prepared to submit to his leadership and authority. There's me all super serious, and super heavy. Clive's reply was 'She's a good'un Matt, go for it!' Simplest, bluntest, best advice I have ever been given. A year later he spoke at our wedding.

Clive had been incredibly moved by a trip to Argentina, and for the rest of his days he burned with a passion for revival in our nation. Through him I began to understand that revival is not a 'simply bless me time' or a 'stand back and God does it all' thing. Revival would be busy and would be hard work. Revival would cost me. We prayed together many times for an outpouring. My enduring memory is of him, at church meetings, with his too-long arms raised to heaven, closed eyes, face up, furrowed brow, beseeching God to pour out His Spirit. One day, the Lord will answer from heaven this beautiful man's prayers. He sadly went, seemingly too soon, to be with Jesus in 2003.

I remember being in their wonderful, architectural masterpiece of a home which was shaped like a lantern and called 'The Lantern', funnily enough. I recall talking to Beth and her eldest daughter Eleanor in their kitchen, when the phone rang. Beth took the call and after a quick conversation hung up, and immediately knelt on the floor. As natural as anything, Eleanor broke off our conversation and knelt with her mother, they briefly shared and began to pray into whatever need had just been passed via British Telecom.

It shocked and inspired me. There were no walls here. No 'shielding' the truth from the children, whilst mum and dad sweated over life's challenges. Instead the doors of life were being thrown open, with tests and struggles being faced together, enabling them to develop and grow up with a reality not just of life, but who God could be in and through it.

Of course, love and common sense prevailed, and the children were not dumped on. They were simply invited into a greater reality.

Why do we so often try to shield our children from life, when the safest place to be is to face into it with Jesus?

Heavenly honesty

Honesty is a funny thing. If someone comes up to you (especially if you are in a church setting) and asks, 'Can I just be honest with you?' Run! No really, get out of there. They are about to use the honesty door as a chance to offload their gripes and grumbles, forgetting that honesty has two sides. Maybe a better answer than running away, which doesn't leave the best impression especially if you are a church leader, is 'Of course, as long as we can be honest about Jesus as well.'

To really embrace honesty is to embrace the tension of living between Heaven and Earth. To embrace my truth and God's truth at the same time. It is not an admission merely of your lack, but an admission of heaven's supply! Too often Christians have ended up plumping for one side of the coin. They are either so earthly honest that it's rather depressing, or so heavenly honest it's unreal and disconnected. Abraham gives us the example of true honesty. It's found in Romans chapter 4:18-21:

'Against all hope, Abraham in hope believed and so became the father of many nations, just as it had been said to him, "So shall your offspring be." Without weakening in his faith, he faced the fact that his body was as good as dead—since he was about a hundred years old—and that Sarah's womb was also dead. Yet he did not waver through unbelief regarding the promise of God but was strengthened in his faith and gave glory to God, being fully persuaded that God had the power to do what he had promised.'

Abraham was honest. He faced the facts. He faced the facts that he was well past it, that 'those' things weren't happening

97

for him downstairs anymore and along with this, Sarah was barren. He didn't avoid these facts, no, he faced into them and went through them to encounter the greater facts. That the God of the Universe had called him and promised him children and a family beyond his wildest dreams.

We have a responsibility to teach our children this by living real faith with them.

Finding faith together

The story I opened with in chapter one, was our first proper foray into this 'real faith' in early 2011. Kathryn and I felt God was calling us to leave where we were and what we were doing, and it was bringing us closer together. This was the beginning of our journey to Highworth via Mozambique and we were praying more, talking about Jesus more, and our lives were beginning to buzz with a greater sense of purpose. This was where this honesty thing really started with the children, we wanted them to experience faith with us. Imagine all being in on this slightly-nervous-yet-full-of-joy faith thing?

It would have been easier to go with the norm and wait until we knew what 'now my child, the time is now', really looked like. Knowing like Abraham (Hebrews 11:8) that God has called you to go, you don't really know where, but you are going anyhow, didn't seem the safest thing to share.

We didn't want to cause our children undue stress or anxiety, but we did want to cause them to experience faith. If faith centres around risk (from our perspective), then how will our children ever come to faith if we insulate them from the realities?

I love the story of Paul sharing the gospel with his recent oppressor, turned seeker, the Philippian jailer in Acts chapter 16. Paul makes his appeal to believe in Jesus to the jailer's whole household, not just the individual, and *'He was baptised at once, he and all his family'* (*vs 33*). Family has always been God's idea, and the cross, if allowed, can totally transform it.

So, we gathered the children in the lounge. They were nine, six and four at the time. 'So guys, we have been praying and God has been speaking to us,' Children look interested, good start. 'Do you remember in the Bible how Jesus asked the fishermen to do something?' (good to bring in Bible parallels) 'To follow him daddy,' one of them chirps up. 'Yes, that's right (win for parenting) and Jesus is doing the same with us, He is asking us to follow Him, and (pause for weight and significance) we think He wants us to move! To sell our house and move somewhere else, but we don't know where that is, exciting eh?'

No.

Ethan looked into my eyes, turned and looked into Kathryn's and then promptly burst into tears. 'I don't want to leave my friends,' he wailed. Seeing big brother take the lead the others quickly followed, and our inspirational faith sharing became a mess of wet eyes, runny noses and tissues; lots of tissues. *'In the world you will have trouble.'* (thanks Jesus).

I don't know if you have ever travelled to the North of Scotland? What hits me is the air. It is so incredibly fresh, unpolluted, cool, invigorating and seems to teem with oxygen. It almost feels like you are breathing for the first time.

Although our first foray into 'honest' faith with our kids, had not quite the storybook start we were after, the coming weeks felt like we were breathing new air. Every twist, turn, encouraging verse and opportunity was suddenly experienced by the whole family. Even Summer, who was yet to turn five, was praying and excited about this Jesus, this Jesus who actually meant we were doing something.

Once you start down this road of freeing honesty, you can't stop - and that's good! Later that year, three days before we moved out of our home and set off for the other hemisphere, I was invited to share with Highworth Community Church. They wanted me to share with the membership my story and take some questions to help them with their prayerful consideration of whether they should offer me a job.

So, driving there, after taking an early shift with the Ambulance Service, I weighed up what I should say. I was aware that employment in a place I wanted to go to, and doing what I believed I was created to do, lay on the other side of this evening going well. 'What do I include in my testimony?' Many of the things that had most impacted my life were within contexts that were, to some, controversial. For example the 'Toronto Blessing', a move of God originating at the end of a runway in eastern Canada in 1994, was not universally accepted or understood. People laughing, falling over and some even stranger phenomena were understandably not easy to process. Excess and misuse had put some people off and turned some against it. Yet for me it changed my life. This move touched many nations and churches around the world and I experienced it for the first time in Southampton. For me it was God in, world out. I laughed my way free of a smoking addiction, selfishness (as my family can testify) and six years of a self-destructive rebellious nature.

So what to say to the church membership?

It's the freedom part of honesty that we easily get wrong. Honestly, there were people very hurt and even driven from church by how that beautiful move of Holy Spirit was administered in some places. Honesty is not forcing my point of view on others. I am not here to tell everyone 'It was life changing for me, so if you don't get that you're wrong!' Honesty has to be brought humbly, and I knew that evening I wouldn't have time to explain every potentially controversial experience. I could only lay my experience at their feet, truthfully and graciously, and 'let the chips fall where they may.'

I guess the evening went well, because five days later I received a very warm and positive phone call from one of the leaders, wishing us all well on our travels and that the church would love to talk more about the possibilities of us moving to Highworth on our return. I felt my vulnerability had allowed us all to connect beyond issues, theology and a desperation to get the will of God right.

Walking in the light

Four days later, we reached northern Mozambique and I faced another level to my honesty challenge. I had decided to blog a daily record of our experience. 'How open and vulnerable should I be?' I knew God was going to work on us 'big time' and I knew parts of that process would be painful and humbling. What would my potential new employers think of me? But once you are on this road, when you are experiencing this beautiful freedom, you know you can't stop. So, I wrote down everything, holding nothing back.

There were days where we both didn't know if we could carry on. It was that refiners fire Peter talks about. The 'temperature' of the cramped living conditions, ultra-basic food (complete with the odd maggot), poverty, people everywhere (we shared a small house with 14 others) and a Holy God at work in your life, meant days of discovering issues in your life you never knew about, anger, frustration, selfishness and oh such pride. I'd thought I was a pretty good Christian. I was wrong.

I recorded it all. Here's a few snippets to paint the picture :

Day 14

Coming here I really thought I had been broken but we are both discovering a whole new level of brokenness. As Jesus said it is the sick who need a doctor, if you think you have it all together then you'll find it real hard to follow Jesus. But here daily we seem to encounter more of our lack and weakness, which is soul destroying and we just pray and hope that God does not reveal these things to make us grovel but to remove them so in Him we can fly. Almost daily I am challenged about why we are here and what we have given up to be here. Will it be worth it? It doesn't feel like it at times especially when the children find it hard. We can only trust it will be. Today I was still recovering from my stomach bug and it was very hot again. Some days we just seem to be surviving rather than moving forward or growing but again all we have is our faith, may it be proved true.

Day 34

Felt myself losing it this morning. Just hit the wall with the water still being out, the electricity then going off, the surprise special breakfast we had to put together for some of the base leaders (wasn't feeling like they should be blessed and rather they should be sorting out some water and electricity) and just feeling I needed a day off. I guess I'm improving in that I can feel myself losing heart and recognise the freefall into discouragement and do something about it. Cried out to God for grace and came in the opposite spirit, I wanted to blame and point the finger but just went low and loved. Really turned around as I reluctantly sat down to the breakfast and let go of my frustrations.

Day 59

Think I'm anaemic. Just got nothing for anything today and I've been struggling for a few days. I spent the whole morning feeling dead, trying to do some chores and pray but nothing. Just want to go home. It just feels like another two weeks ahead of slogging it out and I have not the strength nor desire. I stared quitting in the face. Why not coast for the days left, make it as comfortable as possible with spending all our free time on the beach, surely I deserve a holiday. Yet I believe there is more for us as a family. I know that we have not reached the end of what God has for us here – however hard it is at times. So I chose to continue on if all I could muster was a crawl.

I received a tender email from my Dad one day, maybe four weeks in. He lovingly questioned whether my frank 'warts and all' account of the best and hardest time of our lives was maybe just a little too frank! I understood. You know when you have to fill in a job application and you hit that quandary when they ask you to put down your weaknesses? You know you need to put something down to show insight and that you are self-aware, yet they mustn't be too glaring so as to disqualify you. Here I was filling in my weaknesses list and it was really long. Was it the best way to inspire confidence with a church that I may be moving to, to help lead?

Honesty though, in its purest form, allows others to see Jesus. Paul declares in 2 Corinthians 4 that *'we have this treasure in jars of clay to show that this all surpassing power is from God and not from us.'* I soon discovered my honesty was allowing others to see the treasure. Every time I logged on to update my blog (internet connection was very patchy) someone had commented how they had been inspired and encouraged by my last post. It was in a way shocking. Here we were really struggling, but just sharing these struggles touched people's lives.

It's good to be challenged by those who love us. It is good to check in with any personal course of action and I do thank my Dad for that. Ultimately I didn't continue to be honest because it encouraged people, I did it because it was the truth. I did not want to move forward with anyone holding on to any airs and graces. I didn't want to try to gain approval or fit others' perceptions or desires. If I can be real about me then perhaps I can be real about Jesus. Still today, I feel like it is one of the best things I have done with my life, sharing this daily challenge of trying to pursue Jesus in northern Mozambique.

As we saw with Abraham in Romans chapter 4, honesty is more than just about being 'real' or transparent, it's a vital doorway to faith.

An open door

At the end of 2014 (when we were living in Highworth), like all good families, we took the children out for a country walk after Christmas. But the classic Boxing Day stroll was more that year than just cold grey skies and fits of rain. We shared with the children an idea, and we wanted their thoughts on it.

Since the early autumn that year, Kathryn and I had been looking at where we were really at spiritually and the future. We longed to see God breakout in the UK but recognised how easily our faith evaporated and our passion faded, facing into our dream. We began to wonder if we should take some time out, less of a retreat and more of an advance. A season to give space to God to grow us further, minister to our hearts and work deeper. A time to reach out and practice loving the lost, something that so easily got snowed over by our everyday. 'What if we asked for three months unpaid leave from church, and spent it with our friends at the Iris Global mission base in Cambodia and their work with the poor?' The thought stuck.

So that winter's day we asked the children what they thought about the idea. It was a genuine engagement, our honesty being more than 'here's an idea'. It was and had to be a 'what about this and do you think it's from God or not?' We had visited the base in Cambodia the year before which helped to de-romanticize the idea as we were all aware of the challenges and hardships we would face. Involving the children in this level of decision had to be real and had to matter. If they felt 'No', we couldn't just dismiss that. We gave them most of the walk to think it through and then fedback in the car.

'I will find it hard not being here for Christmas, but I think we should go.' 'I think it will be important for us as a family, but I will miss my friends.' 'Yes, I think the idea is from God, but can we try and get air-conditioning?' These responses were genuine and real. Just because you're ten years old doesn't mean you can't hear God; in fact it is more likely that you do! After all, Jesus has challenged everyone who has ever sought to follow him to become like *little children.*' (Matthew 18:3)

Being that vulnerable, and involving them genuinely in what happened, helped Kathryn and I to step forward in faith. It gave us a starting place of agreement, belief together that this idea was a God thing and, as we found out, we were going to need it. Any dream requires you to embrace the challenges and roll with the punches it takes to implement. Honesty has meant I don't need to be the hero every time. There are days when the faith of my children is literally what has held me and kept me moving forward.

Opening more doors

Asking for three months off work was a rocky road. It wasn't a stipulation in my contract. It was easy for people to read into the request with their own misgivings or concerns. Why do you need a break? Are you dissatisfied with being here? Do you want to leave? Who is going to cover while you are away? All of these, and more, were genuine questions that I understood but weren't necessarily easy to answer.

Alongside all of this we faced a serious financial challenge. We reckoned we needed around £10k for the flights, accommodation, living cost and outreaches and our most optimistic budgeting would leave us a good £7k short.

God dreams have to be stepped into. I have found dream sharing to pretty much always be a tough one, especially when you are putting it out there to a wider group of people. Many times I have shared an idea with someone, something I am excited about, totally anticipating they will catch the same excitement and vision I do, only to be met with a blank stare or worse, a quickfire volley of reasons why it can't happen or shouldn't. You feel punctured, you deflate as quickly as a burst tyre and another dream dies. I am learning that what makes sense to you, as it comes from your personal journey and experience, doesn't always make sense to other people and this can leave both sides feeling let down and misunderstood. Therefore, faith is vital. Moses knew how you and I feel. His attempts to step into his dream (and God's) to see the people set free (Exodus 5:22) were met with complaint and anger from the very people he was trying to help. His dream was knocking the status quo and messing with their comfort. Dreams do this.

That's why you can't share a dream or begin its journey without faith. Faith enables you to share from a place of grace and freedom, because faith is trust in God, it is a belief that God will work, and that things will happen through and sometimes despite how people respond. This kind of faith gives the room for others to grapple and process with you and keeps your heart from discouragement.

The first 6 months of 2015 were a rollercoaster. Rollercoasters are only fun if you believe everything will work and you let go and throw your hands in the air, enjoying the ride. I can remember the children asking me several times over those months 'So are we going to Cambodia?' My reply, 'I don't know but we are enjoying finding out!'

We were all living in between. The Christian walks in a constant tension between the here and now and the not yet.

We opened a "faith" bank account early 2015 with an initial gift of £28 that someone blessed us with, not knowing the financial challenge we were embarking on. Over the next six months we lived the tension to keep moving the dream forward, doing practically and relationally what we needed to do, constantly trusting that at the right time the finance would come in. Money began to trickle in, along with a couple of sizable gifts, as God moved a few individuals' hearts to support us.

By June, with the promises of someone buying our car when we left and paying the rent on our flat, our faith was rewarded. We booked the flights and our commitment became real, moving from the idea to the tangible. We celebrated with a bottle of champagne, laughing as the children pulled faces as the bubbles hit their noses (they only had a taste!), and thanking God for His faithfulness. Our honesty had been an open door for the children to see God work and had given us the confidence to meet the challenges.

The deeper magic of honesty has rewarded us not only with growth together but the move from struggle to rest-filled trust. Recently, I got my first ever speeding penalty notice. 26

years of driving, with eight of those driving as a job, and nothing. I felt annoyed, embarrassed and a little cross at God for not pointing out the temporary speed reduction at the road works. It typically, as such things do, arrived at a moment when I was tired and weary, and we'd already had some stiff challenges to our finances. I shared it with the children. I didn't hold on to it or ignore it but was just simply honest. I had failed, and small though it was it had got me down. They prayed for me, and we put it all in the hands of Jesus. The risk of discouragement getting in was averted, and I felt renewed in God's love for me.

Father and daughter

So, going back to that night in January 2018, when Summer and I had a reality check over our trust in God and our decision to head for the USA. We turned our worries into heart searching prayers and we felt God putting His finger on the story of the feeding of the 5000. Within 24 hours I got a text from a friend, Simon, who asked how he could be praying for us. 'Provision' was my single word text response. Later that day he wrote 'I don't know if this means anything but I felt led to the story of Jesus feeding the 5000 and how the disciples picked up 12 basketfuls of leftovers. Do you have anything leftover that God can use?'

OK God. We had some mountain bikes which we hadn't used for a few years, Lego the children no longer played with and I had an old Marvel comic collection. Now, I am a seasoned ebayer, have bought and sold on that platform for years, know what things are worth but I have never had a time like that. I think the first comic I put on I expected to get £20-35 and it sold for £80. Everything we put on ebay sold well over my most liberal expectation. It was crazy.

Just through leftover stuff we were able to buy five flights from Heathrow to Jackson Mississippi, then on to San Francisco before the return leg to the UK. Wow!

Are you worried about whether God will supply? Summer and I discovered that sharing our worries with each other and with God leads you to a place of trust.

Honesty, it turns out, really is the best medicine.

Freedom. Authority like Jesus himself. Extravagance and Honesty. These are massive challenges if attempted in our own strength, but totally possible if we are empowered by God. That's why the next chapter is so crucial. It's about our closest friend. Read on.

Reflection on Honesty

By Summer

At the beginning of the chapter Dad starts with a story about the challenge of us going to the USA. Earlier that day, we all chatted and prayed about whether we should take the trip and had decided to go, but I still wasn't sure. It would be a lot of money that we didn't have, and I was worried it wouldn't be worth it and would just make life harder. When I told Dad later that day how I felt, I would've preferred it if he had told me not to worry, it would be okay but instead he told me he was worried too and we prayed.

In one way it didn't make me feel better, but it showed me I needed to rely on God, not my mum and dad. Then God reminded us of the feeding of the five thousand and we decided to sell some things we didn't need, on ebay. I remember helping Dad package things up, which took ages, especially the bikes. And in the end, we saw everything sell for more than we thought, it was amazing to see.

Through that I learnt that its ok to sometimes worry and not be confident about things, as long as you can be honest with God. I saw him work through this and I know he can always provide. I had a great time in the USA and I'm really glad we went.

Six

Holy Spirit

'But I tell you I am going to do what is best for you. This is why I am going away. The Holy Spirit cannot come to help you until I leave. But after I am gone, I will send the Spirit to you.'

John 16:7 (CEV)

I was six years old when I was baptised in Holy Spirit. It is probably my first really clear memory. I remember going forward at the end of a church meeting knowing that what had been spoken about I wanted. I confidently asked, a couple of the Elders prayed, and I received and spoke a new language.

At school the next day I told my best friend at that time: 'I have been baptised in the Spirit and can now speak in tongues.' She said, 'Go on then, show me' and in my unashamed 72 month old state I did. Despite walking away from God and years spent disconnected from the source of life this gift has never left me. God gives and doesn't take back.

The issue here however is not the gift, wonderful as it is, but the giver. Here in this chapter I am not going to say 'the' Holy Spirit. It is intentional and not a grammar slip. Holy Spirit is a person. He is often treated more like the Force, than a personal God, in our Churches and in our lives. We don't say 'the' Jesus' or 'the Matt Ford,' so I will talk about Holy Spirit, to hopefully in a small way remind us of this wonderful truth. And by the way, if He's a person then His first name is Holy!

Holy Spirit is God and someone who is vital to not only our lives but the purpose of all creation. Don't just take my word for it take Jesus's.

In John chapter 7, we find Jesus in Jerusalem at the feast of Tabernacles. Here the people remembered their forefathers were once wanderers, homeless, in the desert wilderness for 40 years. As a part of this commemoration, every day, for seven days, the priests would draw water from the pool at Siloam in large earthen jars and process up through the city to the steps of the Temple. Then whilst singing the hallelujah Psalms (113-118), they would pour the water out upon the pavement, in remembrance of God's provision of water from the rock when they were wanderers in the desert, and as a prophetic act heralding the coming Messiah.

On the eighth day, the last day, there was no procession, no drawing of water and no pouring it out at the Temple. This highly symbolic act reminded everyone that God had fulfilled His promise and brought them into the promised land, a land that was well watered and flowing with milk and honey. They no longer needed miraculous provision of water. Or did they?

Suddenly, like the first clap of thunder in a brewing storm, on that day, the greatest and last day, a day of no water, the day when they celebrated their belief that they no longer needed God's miraculous provision, Jesus stood up and in a loud voice declared:

"Let anyone who is thirsty come to me and drink. Whoever believes in me, as Scripture has said, rivers of living water will flow from within them. By this He meant the Spirit, whom those who believed in Him were later to receive' (John 7:37-39).

Wow.

In 27 simple words (in English anyhow) Jesus alludes to being the Messiah, reveals their need of 'other' water that they have yet to drink, makes an open offer to anyone, puts the emphasis on faith rather than nationality or tradition, dispels their belief that Israel was the true promise, and alludes to this water that He gives being transformational, so that every drinker becomes a source for more thirsty people.

Wow in bold and underlined!

Strangely though, to back up such a massive declaration, Jesus quotes a verse that doesn't exist. Nowhere in the Old Testament (or even those extra Apocryphal books) is there a sentence or line that promises that 'Rivers of water will flow from within them.'

How could the God man who so easily, not only quoted scripture, but understood its true meaning and impact better than anyone ever, get it wrong? I think Jesus is going bigger, I think the Son of God is not putting this living water promise out there as a fulfilment of a prophetic word or a single promise, I think he was gathering the entire working of God, every scripture from Genesis chapter 1:1 to Malachi chapter 4:6 and saying everything, all of this, all scripture points to and finds its purpose in one thing: being filled with and to keep being filled with Holy Spirit.

The point of creation is that we are filled with God. The pinnacle of history is you, is me, as the perfect temple, the true temple of the living God, hosting the living God, permanently. This is your calling, this is your destiny, this is the point, the meaning, the fulfilment.

Christ in you, the hope of glory. (Colossians 1:27)

Without this, Christianity is at best a feeble 'friendship' with Christ and at worst a moralistic set of good rules.

Great expectations

It stands to reason therefore that our children being baptised in Holy Spirit is the most important step for them to take in maturing, developing and growing up.

I can remember, as probably all parents do, the moment my first child began to speak. Despite the fact that literally billions of people had already learnt to successfully communicate understandable words via their mouths, I was gripped with excitement and a thought. 'He seems rather young to be speaking, perhaps he is a genius?' Quick internet studies confirmed my diagnosis (probably Yahoo back in those days) he was weeks ahead of the average speaking age and plans started to form in my mind of scholarships, private schooling and early Cambridge degrees.

Ok, so a little over the top, but I am sure I am not the first and certainly not the last! But the real point was Ethan reached and crossed an important threshold. Speech. He would now be able to communicate widely, express his hopes, wishes, concerns and fears. He would be able to ask for directions, grow deep friendships, ask someone to marry him and order a Big Mac and Fries. This and other key developments in each of our children's lives took expectation, dedication, and at times patience. Whether learning to walk, ride a bike, not put fingers in a plug socket, or, now they are older, drive a car, we worked towards and desired these important growth steps.

When I say I expected my children to ride a bike, this is unlikely to garner angry looks that I seem overbearing or pushy. Yet if I say 'I expect my Children to follow Jesus Christ. I expect my children to be filled with the Holy Spirit.' How does that sound?

In our world where choice reigns, this can feel so wrong. If you didn't expect and work towards your child speaking, it would probably be seen as some sort of minor abuse, yet expecting them to be in a vital relationship with the God of the Universe, well that's controlling isn't it, aren't we supposed to give them a choice?

No expectations

A friend of mine was sharing with me a few years ago the sadness he felt that his son no longer wanted to go to church on Sundays. My friend had said to him 'Well it's your choice if you don't want to go then you don't have to.' Sounds fair enough and surely a very common experience for Christian mums and dads up and down the country. I, however, told him that was 'stupid!' (He is a good friend.)

Now, apologies if that sounds harsh and I'll explain my thoughts in a moment. But the background to this is our worship of 'choice' in society. My friend's answer is accepted as common parental wisdom: 'At some point, my child needs to decide for themselves'.

So, answering an older teenagers request to not attend with a 'well, it's your choice', is actually a bad answer. With tears in his eyes he could have apologised to his son for not showing him a lifestyle of faith that was really attractive and worth giving everything for. His reply might have been 'Why don't you want to come? How can I help it be better for you? Son, this is the most important and best thing in my life, I will do anything to help you see that - how can I help you see that? What is going to help encourage your faith and how can I change to help that happen?'

So many children reject Jesus, without ever really seeing Jesus. They often reject our form of Christianity without fully experiencing what following Christ actually means! We only have our children for a few years and that is the time when we pour everything we have into them, to know Jesus. Am I going to let my children walk into an eternity without Christ without me having done everything I can to call them to another home?

I have no desire to be judgemental but please hear me, the question from your teenager 'Can I not come to church?' should never be met with a yes or no answer. There are not only two answers, either, 'Well, it's your choice' OR 'Follow Jesus or else!' Ultimately, your child's question becomes a great opportunity, but only if you are willing to listen and to change. And by the way, if your children are grown up and have left home, it is not too late! Jesus is the kindest person you will ever meet. Be willing to listen, to humble yourself and trust God to move.

All of this is why Holy Spirit is so vital. If you are not filled with Holy Spirit your faith is unlikely to be something others want. He makes our faith real and alive. Christianity without Him is like a car with no fuel. It can look nice but it's going nowhere and is quickly safe, boring and of no real use. In fact, it's more than that. Without the infilling of Holy Spirit our lives are like cars with no fuel, no navigation, no driver aids, no lights, no wipers and probably with no one who really knows how to drive the thing.

I can't underline how inseparable faith in Christ and being baptised with Holy Spirit are. So how did that happen for my children?

Different ways same God

A quick note here. From an early age we made it 'normal' to take our children to great meetings. Rather than get a babysitter we wanted them to experience God's people gathering in different places and with different churches and ministries. This came at a cost to sleep and fuel but has given them a wider view of our faith and created loads of opportunities for them to encounter Jesus. Growing up in the same church as your parents, however good it is, can be hard (I know that first-hand) so this has really helped. We would make an adventure of it, usually involving at least one McDonald's drive through, and talk and pray in the car about what we had experienced.

It was on one such trip north in 2008 to a ministry in Dudley near Birmingham, a place where we had heard God was at work, that something beautiful happened.

'If anyone wants to give their life to Jesus please raise your hand in the air now'. The rest of us had our eyes closed, because that's how we do the gospel talk thing. I had been through the drill many times before but this time felt different. Usually, with my eyes squeezed shut, I hoped someone had their hand aloft, even if they were only stretching, so the evangelist wouldn't feel bad and we wouldn't think the gospel didn't work. But in this place tonight I could feel the power of the message and knew people were going to get radically saved.

'Ok, all those who have put your hands in the air, please make your way to the front.' I quickly opened my eyes to see over a dozen people making their way to the front. 'Yes! Thank you, Jesus.' I then realised one of them was my son! At 6 years of age, Ethan, at around 9pm, in the midlands of all places, responded to the message of Christ. That night he had seen people healed, he had felt the presence of God in the hour and a half of heaven-like worship and he wanted to give his life to Jesus. That night, he got the whole package. He chose Jesus, and without any special prayer or teaching, Jesus filled his life through the Holy Spirit, and he spoke in tongues. He was still Ethan, but more, because God was now in him.

A few years later, during our time in Mozambique, Caleb encountered the living presence of God.

It was hot. The sort of wrap-around heat that is inescapable. The reeded roof offered some respite but the open sides had yet to embrace the late morning sea breeze. We didn't care. We had begun to push our way (gently, as we are Christians), to the front of the 300 plus people crammed into the 'hut', with one hope in mind and Caleb was nervous.

A lovely couple, Jason and Kelly, had come from Ireland to share with our school in Mozambique, on Baptism in Holy Spirit. Caleb, who only recently turned seven, had listened and been attracted by that week's teaching and wanted in. It's funny the things we buy into. For years now churches and church leaders have grappled with 'low attention spans' and the need to make meetings 'seeker friendly' and 'family friendly.' In Mozambique from Monday to Thursday we spent five hours, 8am to 1pm, worshipping and doing church together.

It would have been easy to have given in to my son's worries, easy to have said 'it's okay, we'll ask for prayer later or another time,' but I wanted to model for him 'response', and to show him how to honour what God nudges us to do. He had told me he wanted to go forward, to receive prayer for being filled and so we went together, facing his little fears. Jason came over to us (or more squeezed over), and sensitively asked Caleb why he had come forward. His shy but determined reply was 'For the Holy Spirit.' Jason then simply laid his hand on Caleb's head, with me right beside him, and asked for the fulfilment of the cross in my son. Christ in you.

It was like a bomb went off.

I could feel the power of God hit my son and in an instant, he went from timidity to boldness. His head lifted, his eyes opened wider and he smiled as the realisation of God in us brought a never before experienced confidence, and he spoke in another tongue. He rushed back to Mummy and without explanation laid his hands on her and prayed like a Pentecostal preacher, for the fire of God to come and it did. Mum hit the floor and he went on to pray for others, instantly wanting to give away what he had been given.

For Summer it was simple, maybe less dramatic, but just as transformational.

It was the beginning of 2016. We had been watching the Student Alpha Course together and had just finished the Holy Spirit segment. (The Alpha series simply and deeply shows how the Cross and baptism in the Holy Spirit work together.) The five of us were crammed into Summer's bedroom because it had the best air conditioner.

In the no frills environment of our two up two down home, on the edge of Blue Mountain Slum, Sihanoukville, Cambodia, Kathryn and I laid our hands on Summer (at her request) and simply asked Holy Spirit to fill her. We could feel God's presence in the room and something like a minor electrical shock went through her body, her eyes flew open and she said 'Oh I get it!'

Paul prays for his friends in Ephesus that:

'the eyes of your heart may be enlightened in order that you may know the hope to which he has called you, the riches of his glorious inheritance in his holy people, and his incomparably great power for us who believe. (Ephesians 1:18-19).

He will baptise with Holy Spirit

The church expression I have grown up with was born out of this revelation 'Baptism in the Holy Spirit.' It was controversial, challenging and wonderful.

There continues to be much debate around this issue. Some believe you receive Holy Spirit when you are saved, when you become a Christian. Others see it as a separate happening, something to seek after. Both can be argued for in scripture. In Acts, following the dispersal of believers from Jerusalem, after the martyrdom of Stephen, we find the gospel at work through Philip's ministry in Samaria (Acts 8:1-17). People are saved, demons are cast out and the paralysed walk. Yet, no one has received the personal infilling of the Holy Spirit, and this is something Peter and John address upon their arrival, by the laying on of hands. It was a separate event.

A couple of chapters later (Acts 10), we find Peter, due to some visions and angelic commands, standing on the edge of a new season of mission. The good news is about to break through the 'Jew' barrier and be revealed as for all mankind (thank God). Here at the house of a Gentile Centurion, as a slightly reluctant Peter preaches on the life of Jesus, Holy Spirit falls on the gathering, not even waiting for the ministry time, and Peter and team have to play catch up. It happened as they believed.

And here's the point. It doesn't matter how it happens; it matters that it happens!

All three of my children received differently. But they all received. Do you know that you have received the promise of the Father? Are you convinced that you are baptised in Holy Spirit? If you are not sure, then there is likely something more for you to seek after. If you are sure, then keep seeking after more! The disciples were filled with Holy Spirit in Acts 2 and then again in Acts 4!

Also, it doesn't matter what your infilling experience was like. You don't need to fall over or speak in tongues, but you need to know you are full and you know this because you change! It's not how you are filled but the fruit of the filling! The baptism in Holy Spirit has to change you because it's impossible to be truly filled with God and not become more like God.

'You will receive power when the Holy Spirit comes on you and you will be my witnesses' were the last words Jesus spoke on Earth (Acts 1:8). In Greek the word is *dunamis* and it describes an otherworldly, miraculous strength that enables us to do what cannot be done in human might or force of will. It is the ability to perform and live through God's power.

While I was working for the Ambulance Service, I occasionally had to drive 'the Fiesta' for some errand. The first time I got in it I tried to reverse, as I would in my car and could hardly turn the steering wheel - it was so old that it had no power steering and I had forgotten how hard that made static turning. I was very thankful later that day, to be back in my Mercedes Ambulance and enjoy again the wonder of power steering. Holy Spirit is a little like that. Things we find hard we suddenly find easy through Him.

However this is not primarily the sort of power Jesus was on about. It is explosive God power (the word dynamite comes from Dunamis) and what He, Holy Spirit, empowers us to do is impossible without Him. Faith. Miracles. Perseverance and suffering are all only truly possible through this power.

Beholding and hearing

For my children I witnessed two clear empowerments as they each received Holy Spirit in different ways. They were empowered to worship and empowered to hear.

Worship is what we are made for, everyone worships. We are wired to look for, be impressed by and honour that which delights us, awes us and is greater than ourselves. For many this can be a beautiful view, a stunning Messi goal, or a really good chocolate brownie. Whilst all of these things are great,

Jesus is the one we worship, that we say is worthy of all our attention, who we value above everything else. Problem is we can't see Him.

Without the Holy Spirit worship can hold good sentiment, you may be thankful for what Jesus has done, or recognise the truth of who He is but you don't connect with Him, be in awe of His majesty, receive revelation, or just enjoy gazing upon Him. Worship will always be the preeminent fruit of a Holy Spirit filled life, because He just loves pointing people to Jesus. It's why He came (John 15).

The Holy Spirit brings the weighty reality of Christ to our lives. Through Him my children see Jesus. Times of worship are full, exciting, invigorating and make sense! It is not a duty or something we are trying to work up. We have been empowered to take time to just love Jesus together, and it is such a privilege.

In Luke's Gospel, three different teachings set one after the other highlight, underline and put in bold the massive importance Christ places on hearing properly. You can read about the Parable of the Sower, the Lamp on a Stand and Jesus' response to who His mother and brothers are, in chapter 8:4-21. First, we have the parable of the sower or more truly, the parable of the soils. There were three types of soil: hard, weedy and good. Seed is sown on each of the soils but as you either know or can probably guess, the only one that bore a crop was the good soil and it actually saw exponential growth. How do we be the good soil? How do we receive the seed of God's word and bear fruit in our lives? It is *'those who hear the word of God and retain it.'* (vs 15). We all receive the same seed from the same sower, so the fruitfulness of our lives is dependent on how we listen! A mere three verses later, we are warned to *'pay attention to how we listen'* if we want to be a lamp on a stand, be a source of light to the world around us and be given more. Skip forward to verse 21 and Jesus declares that His mother and brothers are *'those who hear the word of God and do it.'* So hearing is quite important then.

If you cannot answer the question, 'What is God saying to you?' then you are on vulnerable ground. Without His voice we are left to work from our experience, good principles, rely on what has worked in the past, someone else's wisdom or weighing decisions up, listing pros and cons. We are called to something so much more. To hear daily from God.

The good news is hearing from God through Holy Spirit is not something for the spiritual or elite but everyone who has said 'Yes' to Jesus. How? Well, in the Old Testament it was dreams, visions, angels, an audible voice and casting lots! All of that still applies (except lots, that is a little weird now) but we have something better. God in us. The mind of Christ. Holy Spirit dwelling in the temple of our lives, not possessing us but melding with us, developing a relationship that is so entwined and integrated we become inseparable.

Do you realise that some of the thoughts you have are God's thoughts? Some of the ideas are God ideas! He is in us and speaking all the time. It is called relationship and you grow this by humbly stepping out in trust and learning to discern that still small voice.

This is something we have constantly encouraged in our children.

Over Christmas 2018 we were struggling to know what to do about our car. As told in chapter 4 we had purchased via a loan what is probably about the largest car out there, a VW Caravelle, in response to a couple of prophetic words and a desire to mission locally. However it was seriously challenging our finances and we didn't know what to do. The issue wasn't and never should be common sense, but obedience. So, we put the matter to the whole family and each went away to ask God what we should do. This is something we do and you can get some more background and insights into how and why we do this in chapter 9.

Faith is about trusting and obeying God in real stuff, so treating children with real things and valuing their insights grows faith. *'Faith comes from hearing'* (Romans 10:17). Childlike faith (which we all need but children find easier) meant they didn't try to work things out, or let their own likes or fears get in the way, but they simply returned and shared the pictures and verses God gave them. For example one of them was reminded that during their paper round they had delivered one paper to the wrong house. They knocked, no one answered and so were about to leave when they felt to wait on the driveway. A couple of minutes later the door opened and they were able to sort the problem. 'I think God wants us to keep waiting.'

The words were like water to my soul and helped me shed my fears and frustrations and continue to trust in God's provision. Still today, as I write this, we are in the waiting and enjoying trusting.

Hearing God for themselves has not just been important for our children so they are encouraged and know God is personal, but it is a vital part of the ongoing faith journey we all have as a family. Without Holy Spirit alive in each of us, this would be impossible.

It starts and ends with you

Leadership is easy. You just have to live what you preach and know you cannot control what the people you love and serve do with that. OK it's simple but often heart-breaking. We do not live in some Christian utopia. I have many hopes and dreams for my family and my church that haven't come true. I often feel frustrated and confused and wonder why? I want so much more for my family and those I serve. Literally hundreds of times I have challenged and stirred my family for more only to find ourselves a couple of days later back to where we started. I have felt like giving up or wondered if I am doing the right thing, yet, every time I bring my frustrations to Jesus, once I have vented and quieted down, He always asks me 'What about you?' 'What about your heart?' We can't make our children be filled with God's Spirit, but we can turn our finger and point it at ourselves. We can personally always ask, seek, and knock for more.

Are you filled with Holy Spirit? Not, were you filled with Holy Spirit? Today are you filled up? Baptism in Holy Spirit too easily slips into 'the past' event context rather than the 'every day I am dying without Him' context. If you want your children to know God more and hope and pray that they be filled then go after Him yourself. Come alive. Be filled, practise and seek earnestly after His gifts.

You just have to live what you want to see in others.

Being filled with God is the fulfilment of the entire revelation of scripture in an individual's life. It is vital, and we have tried to bring up our children with a healthy utter expectation that it is normal, and it is the best thing that could happen. It has made faith so real, worship a joy and the leading of God through our daily lives a reality, as we continue to hear from Him.

Be filled with Holy Spirit!

For some, like it was for Caleb, your initial experience of Holy Spirit might be like jumping from a cliff into deeper water. For others, like Summer, it's more like paddling in the shallows close to the shore. Neither is wrong or right, better or worse. The issue is 'getting in', steadily going deeper and discovering that there is a never ending wonder and depth to this Comforter, Advocate, Helper, Purifier, Empowerer and Friend.

Holy Spirit is not an event or a destination. He is a lifestyle, a journey, a constant discovery. It's a relationship and, like any relationship, it is far less about how it started and more about how it has grown. We know there is so much more, and, whilst thankful for what we and our children have experienced and known, we hunger and long for more.

In the intimate surrounds of the Upper Room Jesus said this to the disciples concerning the Holy Spirit. *'He will glorify me because it is from me that he will receive what he will make known to you.'* (John 16:14) The Holy Spirit has come to do one incredible and simple thing. Read on.

Reflection on Holy Spirit

By Ethan

Whenever it comes to talking about the Holy Spirit I always end up feeling almost under qualified to say or write anything! I can't remember a time when I didn't know Holy Spirit existed and He has always been a part of our family's decision making process. However, I have never felt overcome by the Spirit of God, I have never fallen over in His presence and I've never laughed uncontrollably. I simply don't have the sort of dramatic stories other people can regale in great detail. And yet even though I have stood in a room with people falling over all around me and not felt a thing, I am still certain that the Holy Spirit exists and is with me!

For me the Holy Spirit is like the wind, I can't see it or where it is going or coming from but I can tell it is there from its result. For the wind you can see the shaking of the leaves and for the Holy Spirit you can see its fruit.

In my life the primary way I know Holy Spirit is with me is through prophecies that I give. My family and I have many stories of both prophecy and words of knowledge, some of which you'll hear more of later in the book. However here are a few examples:

I have told a woman who had been trying to get pregnant for many years that she was going to have a child, having only just met her. My siblings and I once had 4 individual and precise words of knowledge at an event which turned out to be all connected to one woman! And just recently I gave an off the cuff word that many people later said they were really touched by.

All of these words would be completely impossible if it was just me on my own. I have never given a word that someone has disagreed with or been discouraged by because God is in the business of building people up.

This is maybe how I know His Spirit is leading me but it is still far from an audible voice or a sudden trance. The thoughts that eventually become prophecies, are indistinguishable to me from my regular thoughts. The main way I tell whether something is a word from God or not is that it was the first thought I had after praying! It boils down to expecting and trusting that God will speak to this person through me, that these thoughts aren't just my own but are divinely inspired and I haven't been let down yet!

For as much as I delight in seeing people encouraged and inspired by the prophecies I can give them I yearn for more of His Spirit, I desperately desire the types of encounters where people are left on the floor for hours on end, bathed in the presence of God. I know that there is so much more God has to offer and I pray that I will one day experience it!

Seven

One Thing

'One thing I ask of the Lord and this is what I seek.'

Psalm 27:4

In Luke chapter 10 we get this lawyer guy quizzing Jesus on this loving others thing.

What are the boundaries? How far do I need to go? What is enough? So, Jesus tells this made up, shocking story to reveal what, in God's mind, love should look like and to whom it should be given.

So, this unnamed gent is travelling down what everyone knew to be a notorious stretch of road on his own and sadly, but unsurprisingly, gets mugged. Today this would probably look like a few nasty curse words, maybe a punch in the face and off they would go with your wallet, handbag or mobile phone. Obviously, things were less restrained in Jesus time and this poor bloke has everything nicked including his socks, and beaten so badly he is half-dead – I'm not sure which half, but not good either way.

You can imagine the crowd responding with that kind, but world weary, shake of the head. A story all too common for that day. On hearing that a priest, one of their spiritual leaders approaches, their anxious thoughts would have turned to relief. 'Surely here is some help for this poor soul.' But the priest crosses to the other side - puts as much distance from the naked, half-dead man and himself as possible and hurries on his way. And then, next up, a Levite wanders by. A good bloke then without all those priestly rules about dead bodies. This honest ordinary Joe will surely help, but he does exactly the same thing as the priest. What is going to happen to this poor man?

And then just when they think it can't get any worse Jesus says, 'a Samaritan!'

A young child bursts into tears. Young men openly boo. Old men frown deeply and mutter and one older lady faints.

Samaritans were covenant breakers, half-breeds, traitors, bad people. But it's this one who scandalously stops. Wounds are dressed, nakedness is covered, the casualty is transported to a safe place and his long-term recovery is provided for.

Interrupted time. Costly compassion. Radical generosity. Jesus declares that this is what love looks like and it is for anyone in need. Your neighbour is anyone who needs rescuing.

The evangelism problem

To enter this thing we call Christianity, we need to get 'saved'. Sin is our unsolvable problem as we cannot escape it or change its consequences. Someone needs to rescue us and therefore salvation through Jesus Christ is the need of and the promise to every heart through His precious blood shed upon the Cross. *'He* (Jesus) *became the source of eternal salvation for all,'* declares Hebrews chapter 5:9.

In the western church we all seem rather happy with this until it dawns on us that, having been saved, we are then to help save others. We are to be the Samaritans.

Back maybe 16 years or so, I remember making a decision to stop trying to actively see other people become Christians. I was at a conference listening to someone preach a challenging message on our call to reach out, and just felt condemned. I had tried. I forced myself to go door to door, asked God repeatedly for 'divine appointments' and had even been involved in some street outreach. I got that people needed Jesus. I would weep reading testimonies and accounts of marvellous past revivals, but my own experience was a desert of awkward, unengaging attempts and failures to see others know what was so real to me.

Exasperated, I concluded that feeling useless and condemned wasn't helping anyone, so I'd quit the whole thing and just get on with life. Maybe you know that feeling?

I have been in and around churches for pretty much my whole life, and most of that experience has been within the house church or charismatic movement. This movement that began with radical Holy Spirit encounters, young people starting churches in their living rooms with a passion to see people saved, went from hero to zero(ish) in the space of about fifteen years. We got more concerned with doing church than saving lives, until 'evangelism' was something for a select few 'gifted' extroverts. Couple this situation with a general church wide loss of any real belief in hell or living for the glory of eternity more than this life, and I have been left unpicking this mess for the better part of my adult life.

I worked for the South East Coast Ambulance Service for eight years. I was primarily working non-emergencies (better hours) but the highlights of the job were the opportunities I had to do some 'real' emergency work. Ridiculously, the first day I worked frontline we were first on scene to a major incident, where a crane collapsed at a new school build. We arrived to a scene from a Michael Bay movie. Sirens, flashing lights, dust, twisted metal, rubble, panic and screams. That day we were able to save one man's life. He was trapped behind the fallen crane and working with the Fire Service we were able to stabilize him, tend to his wounds, safely lift his broken body through the wreckage and get him to hospital. I exited Worthing Accident and Emergency pumped. My whole body felt rejuvenated because we had saved a life. Someone was alive because of me! It was one of the greatest feelings in the world.

And yet this is what we are called to and more, for every new day that we are graced with on this blue green planet. We just don't really believe it. What if every person you meet today who is without Christ is destined for an eternity cut off from the presence of God? What if this place (Hell) is real and people really do need saving and if the only thing that can save them is the gospel?

So what about hell?

There has been a growing trend of rejection in regard to a 'turn or burn' gospel. The gospel is good news, and a declaration that condemns and focuses on a fire and brimstone-esque damnation is not where we want to be. However, we want to be authentic to Jesus and not to our sensibilities.

One of the major words we translate as hell is the Greek word Gehenna. It's used 12 times in the New Testament and mainly by Jesus. For example: Luke chapter 12:5: *'But I will show you whom you should fear: Fear him who, after your body has been killed, has authority to throw you into hell. Yes, I tell you, fear him.'*

Gehenna means 'Valley of Hinnom' and it was to the west of Jerusalem and the city's rubbish dump. So, when Jesus talked about Hell He was just talking about a geographic place. A valley. Some will therefore conclude that ..... 'Well that's it folks, that's all it is. Jesus wasn't talking about this Dante-like inferno, this eternal place of punishment, just a valley - so let's just shelve the idea of Hell.'

This is not the case! Jesus, as He continually did, took something that His listeners understood in order to help them understand invisible, eternal realities. Jesus takes the garbage dump, a place the Jews recognised as cursed. It was here the people of Judah sacrificed their children to the god Molech. It was a place to avoid. A dark, evil place where things were rejected never to be brought back. It was a place of loss, of stench and decay, of permanent rejection. Jesus takes a powerful image to describe the alternative to responding to God.

Jesus came to save us from something. He did it because as the most famous verse in the Bible states, *'God so loved the world'* (John 3:16). He loves everyone, really really cares for each person, irrespective of what they have said and done.

Along with hell, this love idea is something we struggle to grasp. If God loves people how can he send them to hell? Surely love wins! If Christ's death paid for all sin, everyone's debt is paid? (see 1 Peter 3:18) and doesn't it say, *'God wants all people to be saved and to come to a knowledge of the truth'* (1 Timothy 2:4). Therefore, doesn't God get what God wants? Surely God is great enough to achieve what He set out to do? He is great, and millions of people missing out on relationship eternally with Him doesn't sound great.

The problem is that the 'God getting what He wants' argument ends with God just saving everybody, irrespective of their response to the gospel in this life - it makes faith, the prerequisite for pleasing God, completely redundant. Following this argument means there has to be some option for people after death - that God waits and waits and waits - that there's some sort of holding position for those not in Christ after death where surely, inevitably, like some spiritual evolutionary process, everyone will eventually claim the free offer of salvation by grace.

It might sound nice. But it quickly gets very confusing, completely speculative, utterly contradictory of scripture and based on 'my' created image of God.

In Luke chapter 13:34 Jesus agonises over this very question: *'Jerusalem, Jerusalem, you who kill the prophets and stone those sent to you, how often I have longed to gather your children together, as a hen gathers her chicks under her wings, and you were not willing.'*

Jesus longs to gather the people of Jerusalem, God's children, together, BUT Jesus doesn't get what He wants. Because they were not willing - they said 'no'.

The wonder is that God is desperate for something, is willing to die to get that something, and despite having the power and glory to force the issue, allows us to choose! There's that freedom thing all over again.

That is called LOVE.

In the summer of 1741, a broken, depressed shell of a man experienced eternity and wrote what he heard. In his own words, tears running down his cheeks, George Fredric Handel said 'I saw heaven opened and the very face of God.' This work, 'Messiah', was composed in only three weeks and Handel stipulated that profits from this and all future performances of Messiah 'be donated to prisoners, orphans, and the sick. I have myself been a very sick man, and am now cured,' he said. 'I was a prisoner and have been set free.' Its premiere raised money to release prisoners whose only crime was being in debt. Heaven's music released 142 people that night.

Abundant life

The gospel is not just some epic rescue mission - the gospel is an epic restoration mission! We are saved into something! The promise is not a better life here and now, that's a side effect. The promise is to be with God (and He is really, really awesome) forever!

Jesus said, *'I have come that they may have life and have it to the full' (John 10:10)*. To drive home the power of this, in the Greek, Christ is saying to you:

> 'I have come to give you the same life I have, in all-encompassing excess.'

I have been privileged to travel to some amazing places. Victoria Falls eclipses everything for me. It is astonishing. The mighty Zambezi River plummets 108 metres over this mile-wide falls. Surrounded by lush rainforest and abundant wildlife, it is a place ripped out of fantasy into our reality. You can stand in places where it rains upwards, and I remember being there trying to absorb its magnificence and just weeping. This is Creation constrained (see Romans 8:20). What will our eyes witness in the new Heavens and Earth?

In June of 1994, I was at a student prayer meeting in Southampton, and I encountered the living God. I was filled with the Holy Spirit and words cannot describe the wonder of it. I was unable to stand as I felt waves and waves of life wash over me. I felt joy bursting forth from my inner being, beyond anything that drink, drugs, relationships or accomplishments could elicit. I wept tears of freedom and wonder that I, silly pathetic failure me, was this treasured and valued. And this was just the first fruits, a little taster the Bible says of what is to come (Romans 8:23). OMG!

Do you ever contemplate eternity?

That never ending day when whatever pain you have known will be so overwhelmed by the eternal God that literally life will swallow, will consume, death. It is the place every longing finds a home; every hope is fulfilled, and every dream fully realised. We have the most awe-inspiring future, which Paul declares is better by far, than this present life.

You haven't seen anything yet.

The loss of these two key understandings, that Jesus came to save us *from* something and save us *into* something, have created a gospel that is about this life, producing Christians and churches that live what this life offers, and leadership and parenting that is about being secure, educated, financially independent and healthy. Jesus has been relegated from a Saviour to a helper.

And then Christianity falls apart. The eternal truth of Salvation should be a constant source of thanksgiving, praise and joy, but instead I have often found myself much like the elder brother in Christ's parable, The Return of the Prodigal Son (Luke 15:11-32). I am there in my Father's House (saved), yet it can just feel like a lifestyle of duty, hard work and obedience. I miss the *'everything I have is yours'*, and my joy gets replaced by resentment and self-absorbed judgements. Why did this happen? Why didn't God step in? Why this failure, illness, surprise bill? And I fail to experience the wonder of where I am and the joy of others finding it.

The elder son could not celebrate the return of his brother because joy is dependent on your constant realisation of what you have been saved from, and into, and your desire for the lost to be found.

A metamorphosis

About eight years into my self-imposed evangelistic exile, everything started to change. I'll be honest, it wasn't what I was looking for. I was muddling along juggling family, work, church, finances and the odd round of golf, and then God touched my heart. Flip! You see facts, truths, pithy one liners and even great stories don't change us; they can give room for change or awaken a desire for change, but it is God and God alone that can change a heart.

In the midst of a controversial 'Revival' emanating from Lakeland Florida, God had mercy on me and broke into my life. I went from resentful, dutiful older brother, to joy-filled returning son in seconds. With no plan, or even conscious intent, I found myself talking to my work colleagues about my faith. I suddenly had people asking me questions about life, and I even ended up praying with people who weren't Christians! The things I had sweated to do before, I just did naturally because I was alive in Him.

Now I still find this hard at times, and I can't pretend to be some great (or even ok) evangelist but still today, over ten years since that event, I genuinely want to see people come to Christ, to be there as part of their journey, I am willing to be a little courageous and I am hoping for more. Like yeast, this great commission has slowly worked through my life touching every part.

The one thing

Receiving clarity is a beautiful thing, on any subject, let alone the most important one ever. Those moments are like plunging your head into ice cold water and every sense and nerve is in an instant alive! Hearing Amy Lancaster speak was like that. It was November 2011 and we were sitting in an open sided hut in northern Mozambique. Three hundred of us, a concrete floor, oppressive heat and this fiery lady with cropped dark hair and pink lippy, delivering the sword of the Spirit like a pumped-up William Wallace (except the Scottish lilt was replaced with southern drawl).

> 'The only thing that matters for your children is that they know Jesus.'

It's funny how something so obvious and so simple can be a revelation. That sword, those words, packed full of conviction, and God pierced me to my core. I felt like Saul receiving prayer from Ananias, something like scales falling from my eyes. I actually felt something shift. Since then we have put our time, money, dreams and faith into seeing that happen. You might object - but isn't that the point? Don't all Christian parents want and desire their children to know Jesus and grow in him? Yes, and... no!

We all like to think, as Christians, because we are born again, Spirit-filled, new creations, that our thinking and actions are in line with heaven when it comes to doing life. It's just not true. It's horrendously not true.

We live and breathe in a world that cares not for Christ, and this impacts us to a far greater level than most of us are aware. J.B. Phillip's seminal translation of Romans chapter 12:2 challenges us to *not let the world squeeze you into its mould.* This mould is unrelenting, subtle and disturbingly attractive. Paul is after us having a life on the altar, submitted in obedience to Christ, being a living sacrifice. *'Do not be conformed to the pattern of this world.'*

'The only thing that matters for your children is that they know Jesus.' What if that means the primary investment of your time, money, energy and dreams, is not to get your kids educated, but for them to know and walk with Christ. How would you spend your money differently, if this was really your number one, way above everything else, goal?

My brother and I had a tongue in cheek conversation recently, that I think is actually rather profound (his name is Simon and he has been doing Church youth and leadership work for over 15 years).

'Si, do a lot of your young people pay to get extra tuition or training?'
'How do you mean?' he replies.
'Well a Maths tutor, Piano teacher or Football coach.'
'Oh yes, pretty much all of them. In fact, some may do 4 or 5 after school clubs a week.'
'Si has anyone ever offered to pay you to disciple their child?'
'No. But I was asked to teach them drums!'

Wisdom is proved right by her actions. Now I have no problem with any after school club, learning an instrument, getting ahead or catch up with maths, and I am not looking to start a new income stream. But I do have a problem with our children not discovering a lasting relationship with Jesus. One empowered by the Holy Spirit, to live in all the mess and pain, so they finish their race well. And this will not happen without investment.

Many parents' evenings are spent providing an on-call taxi service, to enable their children to get ahead or maybe get through. The way we spend our money and our time tells our children that lessons, sports and tutoring are more important than Jesus. We value my brother's ability to teach drums more than his ability to guide someone to Jesus.

For many of us the subconscious question is 'What will enable my child to be ok, to be safe, to get good exam results, to enjoy life, to have friends...?' But we need to have a conscious question front and centre through which every choice is filtered:

'What will enable my child to know Jesus better?'

How to 'One Thing' it

Probably the most radical response to this question for us has been to home-school our children for their secondary years. In my late 20s, when I was studying some A Levels from home with the National Extension College, I happened to read an article in one of their magazines. It was about a girl of 16 who had just finished her GCSEs with the college, and I was fascinated to read about a teenager's experience of what I was going through. Their days were focused but relaxed, with parents enabled to be parents and not tutor/teacher. One part that particularly made an impression on me was an interview with a manager at Boots the Chemist, where she had just secured a job. He spoke about how she stood out in her ability at 16 to interact normally with adults. That article sowed a seed, that something different was possible for my children, which bore fruit over a decade later.

So for the last couple of years we have been home-schooling our children. Although Kathryn is a qualified teacher, we are not the teachers. They work using a mixture of online resources, textbooks and paid for courses. It is guided self-study. A 'normal' school day starts about 9am (after paper rounds and breakfast) with the majority of academic work in the morning and more project-based material in the afternoons. Alongside this they get to go to daytime church events like lunches, toddler groups and Bible study, and join us on mission trips.

We have not done this as a rejection of the state school system, or out of fear of the world or a need to wrap our children in Jesus shaped cotton wool. We have made this decision so they can know Jesus more.

This is our response. This is a part of what it looks like for us to bring up our children to know Jesus. It is something I appreciate many people are unable to choose. Our situation is not yours. It is somewhat unique as both Kathryn and I work from home a lot, and the office is a mere 30 seconds walk away. This therefore is not a treatise on home-schooling but on being radical in your pursuit of the One Thing that really matters.

What does it look like for you? How can you shape your home culture as one which prioritises Jesus? Here's some key ingredients we've discovered through this which, with a bit of thought and Holy Spirit help, you can use to shape your and your family's lives.

1. Listen to God.

In Mark chapter 9:31-32 Jesus tells His disciples something very clearly: *'The Son of Man is going to be delivered into the hands of men. They will kill him, and after three days he will rise.'*

Hard but straightforward. I am pretty sure a seven-year-old would understand that. But it says the disciples *'did not understand what he meant and were afraid to ask him about it.'* The disciples' preconceived ideas about their lives, about how God works and how their lives should pan out meant they couldn't understand simple instructions.

Parenthood is one of the best diversions from simple God instruction. So many act like their 'God life' is on hold, that none of that stuff applies any more, whilst we get this crazy-kids-bit out the way. What has God spoken to you about in the past? Are there specific prophetic words you have? Is there a call on your life? This hasn't changed. God knew you would have kids when He spoke to you, and He still said the same things and is still saying them now.

Actually spend some time laying before God your life, your family and what you are doing. Particularly lay down your expectations or the things you think are impossible. Get people you trust to pray with you. Read through old journals or past prophetic words. And then listen. Holy Spirit knows how to balance everything on your plate better than you do. Holy Spirit knows how your decisions now will affect your future. Holy Spirit knows what to do with your rebellious teenager or sleepless toddler. Listen to God.

2. Grapple and review.

This is the working out and walking in the above. We constantly reflect on their home-schooling, recognising the challenges and at times wondering if we are doing the right thing. We have spent many a Friday run (a slow 10k is our thing!) questioning our motives, outcomes and the future. This is good. It brings us to God raw and open and enables us to be refreshed in our faith for what we are doing. What are your children doing outside school? How will this affect them long-term? Does it conform with the vision you have of your family and home?

At a young age Caleb was pretty good at football. Of course, we wanted to support him in this but we tried to look ahead at what a choice now, at age seven, could look like at age 13. Unfortunately, it would look like Sunday mornings, as this is when most kids' sports matches happen. We weren't prepared to sacrifice our regular gathering as church family for this. It's a tough one, but how can I instil a value for the gathered people of God, without actually honouring that and putting it first? This isn't a big stick or religion but a passion to worship as a whole family.

3. Get time.

One of my core convictions, discovered over the course of many years of church leadership, has been that people need time. Lots of time. Despite the attempts of our instant microwave society, where you can supposedly learn anything in a day, nothing of worth comes without a serious commitment of time. And the same applies to our children.

Quantity matters. I understand the concept of quality time, getting intentional moments with people. This is great and being with your children in this way matters but quantity matters as well (I'll unpack this more in my chapter on Sabbath). So easily my time with my children becomes a special diarised event, and we are no longer sharing life. Much more comes out of being and doing together. We spend time at meals, just being around in the house, as well as doing life things like shopping, tidying and church serving. So often I have found a reciprocated new level of togetherness has come just from spending lots of time with them, and there are so many times when, without agenda, they suddenly share openly about struggles and questions. Involve them in what you are doing. Involve them in life.

4. Don't do busy.

Busyness is life being so full that you are running on empty. It is sadly an accepted norm of modern life and one of the biggest killers of faith. I don't do busy. I want to work hard, there is always loads to do but I have made it a goal not to be busy, to always have time to be flexible, to be there for people and the most important things in life. We therefore make sure our children's lives aren't busy. How can they discover themselves, God and who they want to be, if they are rushing headlong from one thing to another? We have actively created an environment that reflects this and keep reviewing our lives so we stay in this. We intentionally keep our lives simple. We do God, work and family. Anything else is a bonus. This even includes our wider family and a whole bunch of amazing friends.

One day, when I arrived to do my Monday morning shift in the Ambulance service, I was shocked to find my crew mate asleep on the stretcher. He had five young kids and they spent every weekend rushing between parties, visiting family and gathering with friends. He came to work to get a break!

Don't get suckered into your life being so full that you are always running on empty.

As I am completing this book we are grappling with the impact and fallout of the Covid-19 crisis. So many conversations and social media posts have been about this realisation that within restrictions many are discovering a better pace and less busy existence. Will it last? An enforced slowdown is one thing, a grace-filled response to life's challenges and opportunities is another. See chapter 10 for more on this vital subject.

5. Put your marriage before your children

'Is this it?' We were on a short break in the New Forest with our two week old Summer, toddler Caleb and four year old Ethan. We were exhausted like any parents trying to adjust to the juggling act that is two young children and a baby. Suddenly and so clearly the question blazed in my mind, 'Is this it? Is this it for my relationship with my wife? Was all that romance stuff over or on long-term hold? Do I need to lower my expectations of love and friendship for a season?'

We both felt we had so little left to give each other and resignation to the pressures of life loomed.

I have often heard parents say 'Well, I have to put the children first.' Desiring to be a blessing and bring your offspring up well is great intent but you will not achieve this by putting them first. In the same way as putting Jesus first is the foundation for a great marriage, the foundation for great parenting is prioritising your relationship with your partner.

Your marriage cannot be sacrificed or relegated on the altar of children.

In a wooden cabin amongst the Scots Pines, I had to make a conscious decision to fight for a passionate and deep, ongoing relationship with the woman I love.

This has looked like lots of date nights, not just one a week. It has looked like us getting away to a hotel a couple of times a year, kids free. It has looked like me learning to cook better food. It has looked like us discovering new interests together; one of ours has been running. I buy my wife gifts a lot. Why? Well it tells her constantly how much I value her, and it keeps my thoughts and affections upon her.

Too many marriages go cold. Too many settle for a second rate version. As a man, I am fully aware of the temptations of our society, the ease with which standards can slip on the internet and the lusts of the flesh. Be real and fight for this thing.

Maybe ten years ago, I remember being in a worship time led by Martin Smith. He started by sharing 'It's my wedding anniversary today!' We all clapped, and a couple of people even cheered. He then said 'and I want to testify today that I have been faithful to my wife every day of my marriage.'

That is a message we need to celebrate, encourage in each other and plan for.

Now, I appreciate you may be a single parent reading this and I want to say 'Wow, you are my hero.' I have struggled massively doing this thing with someone else, so respect and well done to you. I think the principle still applies and I pray Holy Spirit leads you. Recognise friendships that bring life, rest and encouragement and make them a priority. Have a good chat with these people, ask for their help and plan time together.

I pray that the Holy Spirit inspires you to sow into and create a family lifestyle that reflects, within your particular set of circumstances, the ability to Listen, Grapple, find Time, not be Busy and put your Marriage or key peer relationships first.

Jesus is the one thing

I love the word picture that Luke records Jesus painting to the disciples, regarding the spread of the gospel: *'But you will receive power when the Holy Spirit comes on you; and you will be my witnesses in Jerusalem, and in all Judea and Samaria, and to the ends of the earth,'* (Acts 1:8). Like when you throw a pebble into a pond and concentric circles spread slowly across the surface, this good news will spread, eventually touching the whole earth.

History testifies to this truth, and I love those who continue to drive us forward with a passion to take Jesus where he is not yet known. But within this giant sweep of vision, encompassing hundreds of generations, Jesus also gives each of us a personal beginning. Yes, go and help reach the world, but start in Jerusalem. Start where you are. Start where it's most challenging. Start where you live. Our Jerusalem begins with those closest to us. Your family is your Jerusalem. And just like for the disciples, it's a place where you have failed, where you are seen for all your weaknesses and imperfections. Wow. Start there.

To be a witness at home you are going to have to step out of the boat and do something. Read on.

Reflection on One Thing

By Summer

So easily I can focus on what I might have lost or missed out on. Ever since Mozambique my parents have thrown us in the deep end, pushing us to know more of God. Sometimes it annoys me. I think, nobody else's kids have to go to this conference or go to evening meetings, I just want to be like them. Comparing myself to others and my friends and wishing I had a normal life is a challenge. For example, home-schooling has been hard because I feel left out when all my friends hang out in school together or go on trips and I can't go. Sometimes I feel unsure if I'm at the right academic level or if I'm doing enough work. But I do enjoy home-schooling overall, it's just hard not to feel left out. But, I've been able to do a morning paper-round every day for a while now, and it would be a lot harder if I had to rush off to school after it. I've done work-experience during normal school hours at a few places in Highworth, which has been great to do, especially at my age.

I have a faith in Jesus. I actually enjoy most meetings or ministry trips abroad we've gone to. I've got to see God work in people's lives. I find I'm happy to give money away and not just hold on to it. Because we have spent a lot of time praying and worshipping it's become more normal to me.

For example, on a recent mission trip to Senegal we were doing an outreach in Dakar. In the evening we went out to visit two groups of street boys. We were meeting on the beach and some of the team started singing and dancing and soon about 40 boys joined in. They are part of the criminal side of Dakar, a lot of them are on drugs. To either feed their habit or just survive they are involved in illegal activities. They were aged more 15 – 25 compared to the younger boys at the day school.

The Senegalese team there were amazing at including all the boys and connecting with them in a way that we couldn't. Benjamin was one of the team, he preached the gospel to them and over a dozen of the boys responded and knelt on the sand to pray. We could see they were genuine in their response even though other boys were stood at the back mocking them.

It was a good experience and I think it blessed the boys that we were there. It was difficult sometimes, but it was great to give them a couple of hours to feel valued!

Eight

Do Something

'Show me how anyone can have faith without actions. I will show you my faith by my actions.'

James 2:18 (GNB)

One of the happiest men I have ever met was a Vietnamese pastor I encountered while on a mission in northern Cambodia. We were on an outreach on the Tonle Sap lake the largest freshwater lake in Asia, visiting a floating village. Here small homes exist built on barges made of plastic drums, planks and the odds and ends you find made useful by those living in poverty. These people are a marginalised group from Vietnam who rarely if ever leave their watery existence. We spent several hours visiting and praying for people in their homes, ferried by a wooden motorboat, and seeing God do some amazing things as my children enjoyed leaping from home to home across the roads and paths of H_2O. As my Vietnamese is a little rough we were aided by a pastor and wife team from Vietnam. They were a great help that day but the pastor's boundless over-the-top joy did grate after a while and I really thought he should maybe calm down, or be a bit more real. Later that day however I discovered that man's story.

He had been arrested for preaching the gospel in his home nation and had spent 14 years in prison. There he was tortured, rarely allowed to see his wife and first saw his son when he was 13 years old - his wife had been pregnant when he was arrested. Suddenly I had less of a problem with his joy.

Blessed are those who are persecuted

It thrills and wrecks me, these stories of our brothers and sisters who stand in the face of persecution, who *'did not love their lives so much as to shrink from death.'* (Revelation 12:11). And our family's story, the story of the Church, is littered with them.

Just open your Bible to the New Testament. If it's written in English someone called William Tyndale was burnt to death in order that you might read the Scripture in your tongue. Time and again as men and women have taken a stand for Jesus against oppressive religion, pagan evil or controlling secular powers, they have suffered rejection, abuse, loss, imprisonment and even death.

Currently more Christians are facing direct persecution than at any other time in history. 245 million of them.

It is well documented that persecution can alight rather than quench the life of the Church. Tertullian the 3rd Century church father and theologian famously observed that 'the blood of the martyrs is the seed of the Church,' and a towering example of this is found in the most populous nation on the earth. In China following the spread of Communism all foreign missionaries were expelled in the 1950s, faith was outlawed, churches shut, pastors and evangelists imprisoned and killed and a programme of social re-education (brain washing) commenced. Many looking on from the outside assumed the death of the Church in China. Yet years later word began to escape of a Church not just surviving but thriving at unimaginable levels. Through a period in the 80s and 90s over 10,000 people were turning to Christ every day.

On a slight aside, but a well worth it one, a friend of mine shared this with me recently. While he was serving the unregistered church in China, a Cantonese pastor, who had spent years imprisoned for his faith, revealed a startling subject of their prayers.

'We pray for the Church in Great Britain because we hear that you suffer'. Perplexed my friend asked, 'No we pray for you, it is you who suffer.' They replied, 'No, we hear that in Britain you hold meetings and no-one gets saved and yet you remain faithful. That is true suffering.'

Pause, and let that one go deep.

Probably rather stupidly I often find myself jealous of those from whom faith is demanded. When I look at the disciples in Acts the very 'act' of faith in Jesus Christ put them in direct conflict with the religious, with authorities, with occupying forces and pagan religious practice. Their fight was external. They rose up and claimed the blessing of the Sermon on the Mount *blessed are you when people persecute you,* and saw their world transformed.

I weep as I read how Richard Wurmbrand suffered 14 years cruel imprisonment and torture for his faith under Communism in Romania, yet rejoice as he leads person after person into an encounter with Christ, despite the most brutal and miserable experience I can imagine.

I no way wish upon myself or any fellow believer pain or misery, but I do so long for Jesus to be glorified, light to blaze in darkness and spiritual prisoners to be set free in their thousands.

However, the kind of faith that stands against such opposition is currently not demanded by my circumstances. I find so easily I merely exist on a 'just enough' mentality. Just enough prayer. Just enough time spent in worship. Just enough money given, time made available, love shared. Faith in the West is so often an exercise in trying to keep the fire alight, just, rather than building a bonfire that warms many hearts and sets the world aflame.

As John Piper said, 'There is a great gulf between the Christianity that wrestles with whether to worship at the risk of imprisonment and death, and the Christianity that wrestles with whether kids should play soccer on Sunday morning.' (*www.idlehearts.com*)

In a couple of days, we will be gathering as Highworth Community Church for our weekly time of worship. We'll go if we are not doing something else, not too tired or feeling unwell. We might even go because we are passionate about Jesus and encouraging our fellow believers. Would we go if it cost us our jobs, security, social standing or lives?

And if we did choose to go despite these risks would we hold back? Would we be half hearted in worship? Would it depend on how good the preacher was or whether the songs were ones we liked? In no way. We would be all in, hanging on every word of encouragement, desperate to hear from and meet with Holy Spirit.

So, what do we do? Do we try and force persecution upon ourselves? Is that our core problem that faith is easy and comes with little cost? Do we take Tertullian's diagnosis and come up with a simple algorithm for fruitfulness:

Christian + Persecution = Revival?

If so do we catapult some well-aimed offensive social media comments at society to ellicit persecution or do we rage against every perceived sin to provoke opposition? What do we do when it is too easy to miss the point and get caught up in the same things as everyone else?

The forceful

I think we need to realise the nature of the very Kingdom we have chosen to be a part of. In Matthew chapter 11:12 Jesus says this: *'From the days of John the Baptist until now the kingdom of heaven suffers violence, and violent men take it by force.'* (NASB)

In this rather shocking verse (what happened to meek and mild) Jesus reveals the nature of how the Kingdom of God advances and how we are to connect with it and be a part of it. Violence. Fortunately, this is not some Christianised Jihad. Jesus is not advocating fighting and brutality. The Greek word here means to seize or catch up by an open display of force. It's laying hold of something with positive aggression.

At that time, maybe a year after John the Baptist's ministry started, people had been flocking to the Jordan to be baptized, repenting of their sins, foregoing jobs and responsibilities to then go out to the wilderness to hear Christ and then leaving everything to follow Him.

The Kingdom advances forcefully and to be a part of that you have to take hold of it forcefully. You have to do something and let go of something to be in the Kingdom. It's someone who is eager in pursuit, the utter attraction and desire of the pearl of great price and the merchant selling all he has to possess it. The Kingdom advances as its force and power are matched by an individual's force and power. God takes hold of us as we take hold of God. Paul puts it like this in Philippians chapter 3:12:

'I press on to take hold of that for which Christ Jesus took hold of me.'

For Christians living under persecution this truth is magnified. If your faith comes at great cost, then God's pursuit of you is either reciprocated by holding onto Him with everything you have, or you fall away. It's not nice, but there is no choice as to whether you lay hold of the Kingdom - you have to, or your faith will not survive. Circumstance forces you into an active daily walk with God, finding the strength, grace and comfort to simply be a Christian.

Persecution isn't our experience here in the western church; therefore, this verse is key. God is pursuing us, but it takes an intentional, dedicated reaching out of the mundane norms and deception of busyness, if we are to emulate our persecuted brethren and glorify Christ.

Unfortunately, the Christian life is not like some top Parisian restaurant. I do not wake up every morning to be greeted by an angelic waiter complete with bow tie, black waistcoat and twirly moustache, who hands me a menu for the day. I don't get to choose a starter of deep meaningful prayer and worship, followed by a main course of praying for someone in the Supermarket to be healed, a delicious desert of feeding the poor and, if there is room left, a few items from the cheese board.

Hear me. I am not saying grace does not abound, or that we cannot just enter the Holy place, or that the Cross and Resurrection are not the finished work of Christ, I am saying that all of this is worthless unless we choose it.

A few years ago, an Iranian pastor and his wife had the opportunity to move from the Islamic Republic of Iran, where persecution is rife, and the ultra-strict and dark Sharia Law is in place. In the USA they enjoyed the freedom to meet with other Christians, worship openly and reach out without the fear of imprisonment. Yet within the first year, the wife told her husband 'I want to go back to Iran!' Incredulous, the husband asked 'Why?' Why would you leave safety and prosperity for danger and suffering? 'Here in the West,' she replied, 'Satan is singing a lullaby and all the Christians are asleep and I feel myself getting sleepy as well.'

It's time for the Church in the West and for Christian families to wake up! It's time for us to do something.

Southeast Asia

One of my most rewarding 'do somethings' came via our day to day living whilst in Cambodia in 2015.

The local market was set in a cavernous warehouse filled with bright colours, pungent aromas and the echoes of hundreds of voices haggling for their daily needs. It was a place of cultural overload. This was where we shopped, practiced our broken Khmer and felt closest to the 'real' Cambodia.

Dotted every ten metres or so down the main thoroughfare, often obscured by the crowds, were an assortment of desperate people begging. I was buying some cokes for the children one day (as it was crazy hot) and thought 'Why don't I buy a few spares for those begging?'

Three cokes quickly turned into a weekly outreach where the children would make up packed lunches in bags along with some essentials like soap and a few Riel (local currency). We would go and sit in the dirt with the people everyone ignored. They were in desperate poverty, they smelled, were sick, and one guy had his legs missing from a landmine, but mainly through smiles and hugs they became incredibly dear to us.

Our last time with them we worshipped. Despite warnings that the security guards would throw us out, we took guitars and sat and sang with them to Jesus. We had found music so easily crossed language and cultural barriers and there in the packed-out market we did church with our friends. When the security did show up rather than evict us, they joined in and maybe for the first time in its history Holy Spirit moved in that place.

It's in the Bible

My life verses for this lifestyle are found buried in a little story in 1 Samuel chapter 14. Here we find Israel in the now typical situation of having lost the plot, forgotten God and His Law, being oppressed by their enemies and gathering to face a superior invading force, this time in the shape of the Philistines. The situation is all the worse when we read in the previous chapter, that other than King Saul and Prince Jonathan, no-one else in the army has a sword, due to some rather crafty shenanigans by the Philistines.

So think pitchfork rebellion, a bunch of farmers wielding sickles, ploughshares and mattocks (whatever they are). Israel looks screwed. But Jonathan has an idea and slips out of the Israelite camp with his faithful unnamed armour bearer. We read from verse six that:

Jonathan said to his young armour-bearer, "Come, let's go over to the outpost of those uncircumcised men. Perhaps the Lord will act on our behalf. Nothing can hinder the Lord from saving, whether by many or by few."

"Do all that you have in mind," his armour-bearer said. "Go ahead; I am with you heart and soul."

Jonathan said, "Come on, then; we will cross over toward them and let them see us. If they say to us, 'Wait there until we come to you,' we will stay where we are and not go up to them. But if they say, 'Come up to us,' we will climb up, because that will be our sign that the Lord has given them into our hands."

So, both of them showed themselves to the Philistine outpost. "Look!" said the Philistines. "The Hebrews are crawling out of the holes they were hiding in." The men of the outpost shouted to Jonathan and his armour-bearer, "Come up to us and we'll teach you a lesson."

So, Jonathan said to his armour-bearer, "Climb up after me; the Lord has given them into the hand of Israel."'

Well that's a brave decision right there! And a really really stupid one! You don't have to have read Sun Tzu's The Art of War to know this is tactical suicide. To attack a much larger force, at least a 20 v 2 situation, who hold a superior position, and have the high ground, amounts to one of the worst military decisions of all time.

Now perhaps he had spent the night in prayer, asking for deliverance and God had spoken to him? Maybe he had a sneaky rendezvous with the mighty prophet Samuel, who had delivered to him this mission of breakthrough. Maybe. But in an account that is written to show the difference between Godly and ungodly leadership - between those who seek God, Samuel and David, and those who don't, Eli and Saul, it would seem rather remiss of the writer to omit some divine direction.

But wait a minute, how is this decision any different from his father's? Is Jonathan not guilty of presumption and a reliance on his own wisdom as Saul is? This story falls amidst his father Saul's continued failure to seek God and instead act on his own. In chapter 13, Saul 'bravely' offers the burnt offering because Samuel is late, and in Chapter 15 reserves the best of the plunder from a battle with a guy called Agag, for a sacrifice to God. Both on his own initiative for the seeming betterment of the situation. Both are wrong. Big time.

So, here's Jonathan, stepping out without divine direction or obedience to a prophetic command. And then there's the kicker. Perhaps. *'Perhaps the Lord will act on our behalf'* (1 Samuel 14:6).

Now if God has clearly spoken to me, I don't go around 'perhapsing'. So here he is, desiring to see God's people set free from the oppression of their enemies, and puts his and unnamed bearer's life on the line on a 'perhaps'. Perhaps. Maybe. He bargained his life for the chance to see the Kingdom of God advance.

Without fear or a desire for self-preservation, which was his father's failures, and a simple yet deep trust that God was with him, he stepped out. Not only did this result in defeating the detachment at the outpost, who *'fell before Jonathan'*, but in Old Testament terms revival broke out that day. His actions in overcoming one small Philistine garrison caused panic in the wider enemy ranks, and boldness to come upon God's people, so that they rose up and defeated the enemy.

He knew that if someone didn't do something, then nothing was going to happen.

It's in my life

This truth weighed heavily upon my mind recently as I wrestled with my fears standing outside a Mosque. We were doing an outreach, prayer walking an area of our local urban centre, Swindon, and staying sensitive to whatever God wanted to do when we came across this Mosque (I didn't know there was one in Swindon). Immediately it grabbed my attention and I remembered a dream I had had the previous night. In the dream I was standing outside a Mosque, I went and knocked on the door and asked to speak to someone who was in charge. Then in the dream I was invited in. Okay.

This is not a normal everyday thing for me so at first I was trying to come to terms with the literal experience I was having and secondly finding the bit of courage it would take to step out. Fortunately whilst we stood looking shifty at the gates, a man entered and I stepped out and asked him if we could speak to someone. 'I will get the Imam for you,' he replied. Seconds later a young man appeared wearing a traditional tunic and cap asking politely what we wanted.

In for a penny, in for a pound.

'Er, we are from a local church and we were just praying blessings over this area. We were wondering what you do here as we don't know much about Mosques and what happens here,' I explained. A broad smile broke out on his face and he invited us both in for a cup of tea. We spent a lovely 45 minutes there hearing about all they were doing and answering some questions he posed. At the end we asked if he would pray for us. He said 'Well only if you will pray for me first.'

I could feel the presence of Jesus as we prayed and rather than trying to be evangelistic or preachy, we just blessed. I have been invited round again for some food and he would like me to bring my family. Watch this space!

To be like Jonathan, to not settle for the norm but freely step out and do something, you have to embrace a little risk and summon a little courage. You have to be willing to be wrong, so always step forward gently and sometimes the 'perhaps' may be potentially awkward or could be misunderstood.

Something a little different

In the summer of 1998 I was at a youth conference in Newtownards, Northern Ireland. A bunch of us had travelled over from the Sublime Youth Church in Southampton for what we believed would be a time of profound encounter with God. The conference was good, about 200 young people in attendance, but we hit the last night feeling a little flat. We knew there was more. After a time of worship, made all the better with those lovely Irish tones, the speaker invited us to spend some time in prayer and ministry, gathering around different stations. Liverpool St and Waterloo these were not, but there was an area where you could light a candle in prayer for someone who had yet to know Christ, an area for Communion, a place for prayer requests, some stones so you could build an altar... you get the picture.

So we all broke up into groups and with some friends I went and sat around a bucket of water. On it was a verse that Jesus said, *'If I do not wash you, you have no part of me,'* the idea being holiness and washing your hands as a sign of washing away our sins. It was all very nice, and the rest of the guys were praying, but I felt like Holy Spirit wanted to do more.

So I suddenly blurted out 'God wants to touch our whole lives. Perhaps we need to put our heads in the bucket of water?'

Blank stares. Then Dave Boniface (a mate and a great leader) pipes up 'well, go on then.'

So during this lovely contemplative time of ministry, as young people prayed quietly, candles were lit, a few tears were shed and gentleness abounded, I got up and shoved my head into this bucket of water. Dave shouted at the top of his lungs 'Jesus!' and the power of God hit me.

I sort of fell and pulled my head from the bucket feeling alive with the presence of the Holy Spirit. Without another thought Dave did the same, and God filled him. Very quickly our little corner was awash with God (and water) and we were making a bit of a scene. Holiness, we found, brings great joy and freedom.

Fortunately, rather than getting some sort of church ASBO (anti-social-behaviour-order), Mark the leader there saw through the slightly weird wet young men that we were, and recognised God was doing something.

Other buckets and bowls were quickly fetched and before we knew it there was some sort of organised water bucket, head ministry going on, with young people nicely queued to take their turn. It all got rather messy. The water in the buckets quickly turned a deeper shade of pale, as various hair products were rinsed from heads and mixed into some sort of barber's soup. The floor quickly became drenched which was very unfortunate, unfortunate because it was a newly carpeted and the carpet glue began to dissolve then form a foam on the surface, as young people danced upon it.

Nobody cared.

The freedom that night was extraordinary. Post bucket young people were worshiping with unashamed abandon and it was beautiful. One young lad was tearing around the room shouting at the top of his lungs 'Jesus' as he did laps for his Lord. I leant over to Mark and asked him if he was normally like that. An astonished Mark replied 'no, he's one of the shyest kids I know!'

A 'Perhaps' can change lives.

It's simple really

A few months ago, we were spending some time in our Church's permanent prayer space, 'The Upper Room', as a family. It was just a part of our growing norm. That day we had some other things to do and we were all a bit tired, so we had decided to keep our prayer time shorter (normally it's an hour slot). Unfortunately, a couple of other people turned up. A lady from our Church had brought a friend of hers from work and so because we were hosting, we had to stay.

Kathryn was leading some gentle worship and it was all okay, and I thought 'How can this lady experience God?' I leaned over to one of the children and said, 'Why don't you see if God has a word for her?' Honestly, I was trashed and didn't have anything - so when in doubt get someone else to do it!

They paused, then went over and shared a brief picture. She began to cry and God broke in. It changed her life. Opened her heart afresh to a God she had ignored for so long, and I now see her pursuing Christ, a vibrant part of Church. Just from one simple picture. Literally my thought was 'We are here, so we might as well reach for more.' There was no nudge from God or divine inspiration, it was just the glimmer of an opportunity, it was laying hold of the kingdom by force.

For our family some of our responses to this have been simple, like ad hoc worship times in our front room. Watching an inspiring Christian film or speaker. Going to a day conference. Random acts of kindness to friends and neighbours. Stopping to talk and pray with someone in the street. Sometimes it's been bigger.

This 'perhaps' is more than just grabbing a moment by the scruff of the neck. Choosing to do something, to think and act outside of the cycle you are in, is just as applicable to the big life shaping events. Perhaps we should get married? Perhaps we should have kids? Perhaps we should go on a mission trip? Perhaps we should give up our jobs to pursue the call of God? All these and more have started with a question, a thought that is willing to rock the boat, driven by a desire for more, to be more.

God is kind. He confirms and He encourages, but they have taken some guts, some force to lay hold of. Choosing to 'do something' has permanently transformed each one of us, as a family and more.

As I look back on, for example, our three months 'advance' in Cambodia at the end of 2015, I am blown away by how our little Jonathan-like step had such a wide impact. We had the privilege of working with a long-term missionary friend of ours, who is such an incredible example of kindness, faithfulness and love. She is the real deal. At the end of our stay however, she confessed that she had been considering quitting the mission field, yet us being there had helped heal her heart, let go of the past, and give her fresh hope.

I am so thankful for this and slightly fearful. Thankful because it changed us permanently and impacted what we do now. Fearful because it would have been so easy to have not gone, and I don't know where our lives would be now and what would have become of our friend.

Hardly anything we ever do as a family for Jesus comes out of a vision, prophetic word, dream, audible voice, quiet time, prayer meeting or angelic visitation (ok I confess I haven't had one of those yet). But sitting here, on the other side of all we have done, I can see it is God and marvel at how it all weaves together in some divine way, yet at the time it was mainly a trusting step of 'perhaps'.

Traffic lights

One of the things that has helped me have the confidence to step out is realising I had a wrong view of God's will when it came to doing stuff.

Back before the days of online applications and credit scores, if you wanted to borrow any money you had to make an appointment and then plead your case to THE BANK MANAGER. Ties would be knotted, shoes polished and an appropriate shade of lippy applied (for the ladies). The expectation was this would be a challenge - you would have to prove yourself, make a good impression and hope the manager was in a good mood, otherwise your hopes would be squashed. This meeting was viewed as a red stop light, you had to win approval and unless you stepped up there was a good chance of the answer being no!

I think most Christians approach God like that. I have talked to enough people to realise the expectation is a red light on their God plans, hopes or dreams and therefore they are left, sometimes for years, waiting for some dramatic holy thumbs up, a Jesus shaped green light.

What if there was always a green light, and you only need to check it's not red?

This was the challenge presented to me by a radical Dutch chap called Matthias van-der-Steen. He has a big heart for Revival and the poor, has a very cheeky sense of humour, is a good foot taller than me, and just absolutely goes for it. He is passionate about closed nations, places that due to politics and persecution are viewed as a shut door to the purposes of God. For example, in 2012 I was privileged to be part of his team taking the gospel to Myanmar. We held huge meetings where thousands were healed and gave their lives to Jesus. I personally got to baptise 24 people one night and I was only one of about 20 people baptising! I have never seen so many people respond to the gospel in such a deep and meaningful way. The crazy thing was that had we conducted these meetings five years earlier, we would have all been deported and the local church leaders imprisoned. Matthias had been working in that nation with heroic church pastors for years to bring us to that point. His expectation is a green light, a go on his God plans - he just checks it's not red.

Jesus has already died on the cross and been resurrected to life. The Holy Spirit has already been poured out to empower His people. As Paul puts it in 1 Corinthians chapter 1:20-22:

'Whatever God has promised gets stamped with the Yes of Jesus. In him, this is what we preach and pray, the great Amen, God's Yes and our Yes together, gloriously evident. God affirms us, making us a

sure thing in Christ, putting his Yes within us. By his Spirit he has stamped us with his eternal pledge—a sure beginning of what he is destined to complete.' (The Message)

This is not some carte blanche to do whatever you want. Humility is crucial. You must be free of agenda, ambition and selfish wants and willing to hold things lightly, seeking the hand of God as you step out. But we approach a God who loves our world and wants to use us to transform it. We come with open hands, not clinging to our plans or dreams, willing to let them go, or let them die. We just need to check that its ok to go for it and what His timing is.

Humility for us is the Dr Pepper principle. We ask ourselves 'What's the worst that could happen?' If we are happy to pay the price to that question, then we go for it, and whether the steps we are taking are big or small, we are willing to get it wrong and pay the price. The great news is, even when I do get it wrong God is still good.

And it's this goodness that is our confidence moving forward. He is a perfect Father who catches us when we fall and turns even my failures to His glory. What we find when we step out and we do something that goes against the flow is a really, really, really good God.

So, do something. Disturb the waters of your day to day.

But how does this affect my family? What does this mean for bringing up children or for those I am discipling? To do something you sometimes need to get a little pushy. Read on.

Reflection on Do Something

By Ethan

As I reflect on the idea of 'doing something' I think we all get a particular picture in our heads as to what that means. Some of us might think of missionaries like Heidi and Rolland dropping their entire lives to pursue God in the slums of Mozambique or others might think of Mother Theresa laying down her life for lepers in India, but I think one of the key things that I have been taught over the years is that God's work isn't just exclusive to those who can give up everything. God's work is anything that can bring other people closer to Him!

A good illustration of this is the difference between a thermometer and a thermostat. A thermometer is dictated to by the temperature of the air around it, while a thermostat actively changes that temperature. In the same way we can do something. Doing something can be as simple as trying to increase the spiritual temperature of the room. This can range from being a calm voice in a stressful situation to praying when no-one else wants to! All of it can create an example for others to follow and create an atmosphere of God's love.

While we were in Ghana we met a missionary called Sue Kolljeski. She had a name for this type of 'doing something', she called it the ministry of presence. The idea is to bring Gods love and peace to every situation that you find yourself in and show the world an example that can point them to Jesus.

A brilliant example of this came during our Ghana trip when, as we were staying with her, Sue received word that an important member of a nearby village had died. As it was sub-Saharan Africa they didn't have the means to keep the body for any length of time so the funeral was being held that day. Sue decided to go to the funeral and asked if we wanted to join her. So soon we found ourselves in a crowd of a few hundred people as hired mourners wailed in the background. The deceased was propped up in a canopy surrounded by his spears and shield, with his wife wandering around tied with a leash! This was definitely unlike anything I had ever seen before. We were deep in the area of Africa where voodoo originated and witchdoctors still hold sway. Their customs were strange and the atmosphere was dark. However despite the distinct feeling of being a fish out of water, we persevered in staying there and even requested if we could pray with the family. When our request was granted, we knelt in the dirt with the wife and her three children, people whose lives had just fallen apart around them, losing their only stable income and protection.

We prayed hard that day. We prayed for the wife, the children and we prayed as we sat in the plastic chairs scattered across the area of mourning. Dad even went out and stood before the body, boldly praying not for peace but instead for resurrection! There was no Lazarus that day, but as we travelled around the gathering and prayed with the family, we were able to bring a small light of hope, a glimmer of peace and the hint of a smile to them. It wasn't that hard. We didn't lose or risk anything in what we did and whilst we haven't heard of any miraculous revival breaking out because of our prayers, if we hadn't prayed with them or gone to that funeral, that family would have been left with nothing but grief, sadness and darkness. Too often when we consider whether we should do something, we think of the cost to ourselves, instead of the light that we can bring to those around us.

I've learnt that following Jesus means not settling for what we see around us and instead being prepared to step out and bring Gods light into any situation.

Nine

Push Them

'And let us consider how we may spur one another on toward love and good deeds,'

Hebrews 10:24

'Hey guys, what if we did some words of knowledge?' We were thirty minutes out from arriving at a CAP (Christians Against Poverty) event in the New Forest and I had been racking my brains to think of a way of involving our children. This was something of a new venture for us as a family. Kathryn had been working for CAP nationally as a regional evangelist for about 18 months or so, and about once a month she got to go and share the gospel with a CAP centre's clients at an event like a curry night or pamper evening. It was one of those things she said 'Yes' to because she felt the nudge of heaven, despite feeling utterly inadequate.

On a very quick aside, if you don't know about CAP then do find out. They are an amazing international charity, run from that spiritual hotbed Bradford, who offer free, professional debt advice to anyone. They have a massive passion for Jesus and the practical love they give, mainly to people outside of the church, has seen hundreds come to a saving faith. It's a way of seeing the kingdom of God touch lives in our nation and support the Church on her mission.

Back to the New Forest. Kathryn had always gone to these events on her own, so this was the first time we were all going, with permission from CAP, to try and share as a family. But how do we all get involved?

Words of knowledge are a Holy Spirit gift (1 Corinthians 12:8) that can help people experience the God who knows and cares for them. You receive information about a person through the Holy Spirit, information you had no other way of knowing, and then share this in a grace filled way, thus creating an opportunity for people to encounter God. The occasion of Elisha's interaction with Naaman in 2 Kings chapter 5 and Jesus' insights into Nathaniel in John chapter 1 are a couple of good examples of this gift.

Now, despite the odd moment of prophetic clarity, as you will shortly see, this was not something we had ever intentionally done ourselves or been on a training course for. We had done 'prophetic words' together but not this; still it was my only idea. I was confident that the children were used to hearing from God, so why not take another step?

On arrival we got a few minutes to pray together and I just said something like 'Let's ask the Holy Spirit to come and then wait. We are expecting God to share some information that helps highlight who He wants us to minister to. Maybe it will be an illness, an area of the body that is in pain, a name or a picture. Don't over think it and we'll just go with whatever pops in our heads.'

There we are, training done. We prayed and then all shared what we had.

The gifts of the Holy Spirit are just that, gifts! They are presents from God and should be experienced, shared and received with freedom and joy. It's an incredible blessing and faith builder to hear God speak through people and often sharing what you receive wisely and gently from the front of a meeting does that. Sadly, I have seen the gifts abused, used like a club to break and demolish, rather than creating a Christmas Day round the tree experience. If God gives you something very personal for someone you don't share it openly from the front of a meeting. You ask God what He wants you to do with it - maybe it's just to be praying for that individual. Gifts by nature are wrapped in kindness and love - wrap your gifts in kindness and love!

So, we shared with each other what we felt from God. Caleb had 'Problem with right knee,' Summer had the name 'Lucy', Ethan had 'a Problem with selling your house or with moving to a new house,' and I had a picture of a 'red jumper.' This was all before anyone arrived.

Later at the end of her talk, Kathryn told the thirty or so present that we had been praying for them all and God had highlighted a couple of things to us. Problem with your right knee, the name Lucy, difficulty selling or moving house and someone wearing a red jumper. 'If any of this makes sense to you, we would love the opportunity to pray with you.' That was it, low key and brief.

Five minutes later a lady approached Kathryn. 'I have never been to something like this (she was unchurched) and I don't know if it's me but I have arthritis in my right knee, my dog's name is Lucy, I have had my house on the market for some time with no success and I am wearing a red jumper.' 'I think it probably is,' Kathryn replied with a smile on her face.

That night the children prayed for her and all the pain left her knee and she was able to walk on it like she hadn't for months. That night we pus hed them to go further and something great happened. C'mon.

A pushy God?

Being a pushy parent sounds awful, but we all do it, just not necessarily with faith. What parent has not been 'pushy' regarding a child doing their homework, tidying their room, attending the club they have paid for, or apologising to someone they have hurt? We are supposed to push them, to encourage them and expect them to step out, grow and fulfil the responsibilities they have committed themselves to.

Why? Well, because that's what God is like.

In Acts chapter 9, in the great city of Damascus, a man briefly, yet significantly, enters the story of the outward growth of the gospel and the annals of church history.

This man, Ananias, had a vision. Jesus spoke to him. 'Yes Lord,' was his confident, here I am for you, reply. And then Jesus asks him to go and pray for and heal Saul. Ah. The guy who had not only threatened the slaughter of Jesus' followers but had been given the authority to carry out those threats. Ananias remained calm (ish), took a deep breath and then reminded God, in case he had overlooked the facts being busy running the universe and all, that this Saul was not a good guy and going to him would jeopardize his own safety.

But the Lord said 'Go.' And so, he did. In an act of great courage and great forgiveness, he greets Saul as brother and sees him healed and baptised in the Holy Spirit. This Saul became Paul the great missionary, revivalist and writer.

The biblical God is quite pushy it would seem. He is constantly calling people to step out, go through perceived barriers, give up stuff, change direction, do something different, face their fears, go where they don't want to and quite often put their lives on the line doing all the above.

Imagine being Zebedee (Matthew 4:21). Business is going well, and you are just preparing to go out fishing with your two sons, who you had spent years training to continue the family business. Then some bearded Rabbi walks by, calls James and John to fish for men, and you find yourself alone, your plans up in smoke! And don't get me started - pretty much every person in the Bible that walks with God, from Noah to Peter and Gideon to Philip... all of them experience a God who pushes them.

This God doesn't seem to have a big place in the lives of our families and our churches. Faith today is cotton wool covered. Safe. Constantly watered down so as to not offend and be too challenging or demanding. We focus on the nice bits, Jesus loves us, is for us, forgives us and has grace when we fail. No one, as George Verwer remarked recently at our church, says their favourite Bible verse is Christ's words in Luke chapter 14:33:

> 'If any of you does not give up everything he has he cannot be my disciple.'

If you are going to see your children go after 'One Thing', after Jesus, and 'Do Something' for Jesus that goes against the flow, seeing light break into darkness, then just like Jesus did with His disciples, we are going to have to push them.

And in fact, the Bible commands it:

> 'And let us consider how we may spur one another on toward love and good deeds, not giving up meeting together, as some are in the habit of doing, but encouraging one another - and all the more as you see the Day approaching.' (Hebrews 10:24-25)

The word here for spur means 'to wound in order to illicit a response.' Now I am not at all advocating getting physical, but that our words and expectations should shake our children into action. We are supposed to have a heavenly culture of challenge, like a PT instructor encouraging us to do one more rep; they know we can do it, we think we've reached our limit but they help us take another step beyond.

Build people up

Pretty much the entirety of what it looks like to be a part of church is summed up in the one word, encourage. The word is from the same root as the word the Bible uses for Holy Spirit, which is fascinating. The word Jesus uses in John chapter 14 and 15 to describe Holy Spirit, we translate as helper, counsellor or advocate. The word means to come close beside and make a call. Someone who is close enough to you to make a correct judgment call about you. It was a term used to describe a lawyer; a person employed to make a stand for your rights. This is what Holy Spirit does. He is so close He is in you, knows everything about you, and who you really are in Christ. He then constantly works to call, encourage and challenge you into Christ, into the person you were reborn to be. We are all called to be like little Holy Spirits to each other. We are to come alongside each other and point each other into what we are called to be.

It's not about a worldly pushiness that is heavy, achievement driven or laden with our own ideas. It's calling our children to be all that they can be in God. We encourage them, that they may encourage others. That is the core of discipleship and parenting. These verses are for parents and for families to walk in. The commands and wisdom of the Bible are not just for church stuff or some elite disciples. Let's tear down the curtain separating all the Bible's truth from family life. The writer to the Hebrews implicitly expects us to spur our children on, creating in them good habits, in an environment of encouragement.

And that's the point. Creating new habits. Our children will happily encourage someone through prayer and prophecy at the drop of a hat now because pushing them has created a habit of being engaged and hearing from God. This is what 'godly pushy' is all about.

The idol of choice

Bringing up your child to know Jesus is hard. Mainly because you can't make them do it. I remember pouring my heart out to my Colour Group (think home group with more sacrifice) in Mozambique, feeling the weight of desire for my kids to walk big and free in Christ, and yet wallowing in the realisation that I couldn't make them. Teaching our kids how to wash their hands, not stick knives in plug sockets and put their shoes on (thank God for Velcro) is something we 'make' them do, gently, with occasional bursts of foot-putting-down ultimatums. Giving Jesus your life and following Him cannot be forced, but what we can't do is just leave it to them. This supposedly wise view that we must let our children decide what they want for themselves is ridiculous. I am not leaving their eternal destiny to them without doing everything I can to encourage and push them into Jesus.

Choice has become the greatest commodity (right or desired goal) in our society. The continual elevation of the individual has naturally resulted in our supposed ability to now choose...everything. From your gender to the hospital you attend for surgery. Choice is king. However, no one has the freedom of real choice because none of us exist in a vacuum. Everyone else's choice affects ours and we are all influenced and pressured to make choices in the direction we are positioned, in relation to what we like, or where we feel accepted.

I was sitting in my ambulance (previous job), having just parked up at the station early for once. My crew mate, knowing I was a Christian, suddenly bursts out with 'Don't you think you have been brainwashed?' Often, I meet these moments in the complete opposite way from our Lord and fumble out some bland statement that I am left kicking myself about later. But this time the answer came without a thought, it came from somewhere deep. 'I understand what you are saying, but I live in a world that constantly bombards me with a belief that is completely opposite to mine. Adverts, films, magazines, social media, everywhere I go I am told things that are different from my own beliefs and opinions. The fact that I survive with my faith intact is a miracle and surely if anyone is brainwashed it's, well....... everyone else.'

A big part of being this disciple making parent, that spurs our children on into Jesus, is about creating a culture where our children can make great informed choices, free of the conforming influence of the world. That is what this book is all about. We have to push them into living 'our real life' walking with Jesus, not a nice idea and a set of church meetings.

Trained and Going Nowhere

At 19 years of age I was in Malawi with YWAM (Youth with a Mission) and I was shocked at how I understood more of the Bible and had a better theological grasp of God than nearly everyone in the 800 person strong Church we were serving for six weeks. But I was more shocked at how much better they were doing this Christian thing than I was. They gladly fasted, made sacrifices, praised for hours, prayed all night every Friday, and saw miracles on a weekly basis.

We are the most highly trained and informed generation there has ever been, yet we are ineffectual because we don't live it and that's what our children need.

There's this crazy bit in both Matthew's and Luke's Gospel. We call it 'The Lord's Prayer.' In Luke's account in chapter 11 the disciples approach Jesus after He has finished praying and ask Him to teach them to have the same relationship with Father as He does (that's the point of a prayer life by the way). As Bill Johnson points out, 'They had seen Jesus feed the five thousand, but they don't ask Him to teach them to multiply food. They had seen Jesus calm a storm, but they didn't ask Him to teach them how to control the weather, (although this would be helpful for us in the UK). They see Jesus heal the sick but again they do not ask Him to put on a healing course. But when they see Jesus pray, they ask Him to teach them that.' (www.ibethel.org)

The wonder of Luke chapter 11 is Luke chapter 9. Before they had any prayer training or maybe even any idea how to pray, it says this:

'When Jesus had called the Twelve together, he gave them power and authority to drive out all demons and to cure diseases, and he sent them out to proclaim the kingdom of God and to heal the sick. He told them: "Take nothing for the journey—no staff, no bag, no bread, no money, no extra shirt. Whatever house you enter, stay there until you leave that town. If people do not welcome you, leave their town and shake the dust off your feet as a testimony against them." So, they set out and went from village to village, proclaiming the good news and healing people everywhere.'(vs 1-6).

Before they even knew how to pray!

We know the disciples were young. In Matthew chapter 17:24-27 only Jesus and Peter pay the temple tax by some rather nifty fishing. This was a tax that all men had to pay who were aged 20-50 years old in Israel, thus indicating all the other disciples were likely just teenagers. So in Luke chapter 9 Jesus sends out this untrained and inexperienced bunch of lads in their teens and twenties, who have the audacity to just believe and follow simple instructions, and it works. This is Jesus pushing them to live the kingdom and it results in their desire to learn more. The *'teach us'* came directly out of their experience of living out the gospel.

God turns up at a shrine

'You can't have children, but if we pray, God is going to give you a baby!' This was one of the first words of knowledge my eldest son Ethan ever had. He was 13 years old and we were in Cambodia as a family. A spare afternoon had given us the chance to 'go and see what God wanted to do.' So, we had prayed, felt a spiritual hunch to head to a local shrine that was a short moto ride away in a local park and spend some time worshipping.

In the lazy afternoon heat of the park we found a large rock to sit on, and with the shrine behind us, we sang some 'God songs' as old ladies wandered by, children ran by, a fleet of tai chi aficionados did their thing and a couple of beggars eyed us warily. A Khmer (local) lady who was passing by stopped, and at a safe but interested distance, she listened to our worship, obviously moved by God (or shocked by my voice). After a few minutes, my wife Kathryn approached her while the kids and I prayed, not knowing what they were talking about.

Fortunately, she knew 'good English' as she was married to an Australian. She soon began to pour her heart out to Kathryn, sharing her longing to be a mum, yet after years of trying her fear was that her barrenness would result in a broken heart and a broken marriage. This was when Ethan wandered over and whispered in Kathryn's ear what he felt God was saying. He had been too far away from the conversation to overhear anything. Kathryn then shared this with the lady who wept because for the first time in her life Jesus was making himself known. There was a God, He knew her and wanted to do great things in her life. We all got to pray for her. We forgot to get contact details to find out what happened, but I know Jesus is not in the habit of revealing empty promises through children.

Faith = belief in action

And this I guess is the point of the book. If you want to bring your children up to know Jesus, then do stuff. Don't just teach them Bible stories, live Bible stories. Ethan had had zero training in words of knowledge. But he had Christ in Him. He didn't know that prophesying that sort of thing was for the professionals, or an end result of years of prophetic development. All he knew was you listen more to God than to the other voices and that nothing happens if you don't do something and obey.

The goal is for these things to create a culture in you and in what you do. The goal is a new normal, a new culture for you, your family, your ministry or your church. We don't have to spend time daily 'pushing' our children because the culture creates an expectation. It's normal. We expect them to be involved and they expect to be involved.

Recently, we were in Senegal sharing with some missionary friends about doing missions and living faith as a family, something of the substance of what's in this book. They are a fantastic missionary family with younger children and they asked our kids how this had been for them! Ethan who was 17 at the time, shared about growing up in a culture of being pushed. 'Way back when we were in Mozambique, dad started talking about being all in. He would challenge us seemingly constantly about putting everything you have into what you are doing for God. There have been times when this has been hard, and I didn't really want to hear it. However over time I have realised that this persistence has meant I now do these things without thinking. I am naturally engaged and all in. Challenge your children, even if they don't seem to want it because it works, and I am thankful my parents did.'

Being passionate is good. Being driven just leads sooner or later to a crash or burn out. What enables us to consistently step out, whilst pulling and encouraging others to come with us, without ending up a wreck? Read on.

Reflection on Push Them

By Caleb

I guess it's just been normal.

Growing up with a culture of being challenged by my parents, not in a judgemental way, but with them coming alongside and encouraging me to do something more. Starting from a place of knowing that they want me to go further in my walk with God than they have, and knowing the challenge is out of love not judgment, I can take it to heart and am more able to act boldly and in faith.

I find it easy to be satisfied with my life where I'm in control doing what I want to do and not really taking action within my life in God, and maybe you have too, but when we feel like this do we need to question that if there aren't struggles, are we doing the Christian life right?

That's not to say I'm directly disobeying God's word or sinning against him, but it is the reality that the Bible says walking with God is meant to be a joyful, wondrous and active journey. I confess that I haven't always been active in my journey, but I've found that a big part of being able to 'push' others and encourage them further, is being able to be pushed myself.

I hate to break it to you but likely most of the time you won't feel like stepping out in faith, or you won't want to be pushed by others, I know I definitely didn't and probably still don't, but that right there is the challenge. To be willing to have someone say to you 'Hey, why don't you share a word?' or 'Why don't you give someone a prophetic word?' not to dismiss it instantly, to know you don't want to do it and you'd rather do anything else, but to take that step in faith that God will use you.

God isn't in the habit of letting down those who put their trust in him, he always comes through, if maybe not in the way you think.

As my father has said many times when encouraging me and my family to do something we might not want to do, 'What's the worst that can happen?' When you share a word with someone, to a group of people, or even a whole congregation, 'What is the worst that could happen?' You might embarrass yourself? Or maybe you get it wrong and then you're led to think that you just can't do it?

I remember a time when I stepped out and shared a word to a group of people, I stumbled over my words and couldn't really remember what it was I was trying to say. I thought it was a complete disaster and wanted just to disappear, but when you really stop and think, it isn't the end of the world if it doesn't work how you wanted it or planned. My job is to try, and to say yes, and leave the rest up to God.

I want to end with this: *100% of the times you don't step out or let yourself be prompted by a person or, perhaps more importantly God, nothing will happen.*

How can it? How can something happen when there's no-one there to help engineer it?

I've missed opportunities that I should've taken and will probably miss some in the future, but that's the wonder of God, he always gives second chances and is always ready for me to engage if only I am willing.

Ten

Sabbath

'Let us, therefore, make every effort to enter that rest, so that no one will perish.'

Hebrews 4:11

From a huge mountain cloaked in billowing smoke and drenched in fire, God speaks to a mass of a million or more refugees.

'I am the Lord your God who brought you out of the land of Egypt, out of the house of slavery' (Exodus 20:2)

Here in the fearsome and awe inspiring birth of a nation in amidst deafening trumpet blasts, smoke, flames, an entire geographic feature bathed in thick cloud and the audible voice of God, it's easy to forget where the Israelites had come from. It's easy amidst the non-stop action of Exodus with its encounters, flaming bushes, plagues, resistance, boldness, escape, pursuit and salvation to forget bricks.

Bricks. It was all they had known and was the only job the Israelites had held for as far back as they could remember. Brick making. This sea of people had been slaves, tasked with helping build the architectural wonders of Egypt by making bricks. Every single day. All week and all year. Their parents made bricks, their grandparents made bricks, their grandparent's parents made bricks, in fact for the last 400 years all the family had done was make bricks. All day. Every single day.

The world of Egypt had shackled the Israelites with an impossible workload that consumed all their time and all their energy. Egypt biblically represents the world. A system and culture that consumes your time, focus and energy with you at the centre - it's all up to you - it's all about you, and rest, real rest, is a mirage-like dream.

And so God speaks in Exodus chapter 20 and we get these Ten Commandments that we can view as a list of rules, God laying down the law. But before any of this is uttered God tells them that He is their God and He sets them free, and with this one sentence the entire emphasis shifts from rules and laws, to commands that enable the people to live in this freedom!

The Ten commandments are about freedom!

These are not ordered to restrict, control, or make your life boring, they are revelations of God's heart and, if responded to, enable us to live in true freedom. There is no freedom without law. And so - with His own finger - God carves out a new way of living - the Ten Commandments:

1. Do not have any other gods before God.
2. Do not make yourself an idol.
3. Do not take the Lord's name in vain.
4. Remember to keep the Sabbath day holy.
5. Honour your mother and father.
6. Do not murder.
7. Do not commit adultery.
8. Do not steal.
9. Do not bring false witness against your neighbour.
10. Do not covet. (lust after/be envious of)

As was common regarding expectations of any covenant at that time, God gave His covenant in the order of priority toward Him. The first five commands are about heart, they are about relationships. They establish a foundation from which the justice of not killing, stealing etc. could be performed. Without the first five none of the next five can be truly obeyed, as they should, from the heart.

Four and five

Generally I have had little problem, at least in theory, agreeing with the last five or the first three. On the surface taking a day off and being nice to mum and dad, obeying the commands of Sabbath and Honour, has been relatively easy to follow as well. Yet in recent years God has led me on a journey with these two commands allowing some beautiful insights into the heart of God, things that I had previously not understood nor practised. 'The deeper magic' I have found has radically reshaped my life and I am excited to share this with you, starting with some insight into this whole Sabbath thing.

The fourth command interestingly is the longest. Exodus chapter 20 vs 8:

'*Remember the Sabbath day by keeping it holy. Six days you shall labour and do all your work, but the seventh day is a sabbath to the Lord your God. On it you shall not do any work, neither you, nor your son or daughter, nor your male or female servant, nor your animals, nor any foreigner residing in your towns. For six days the Lord made the heavens and the earth, the sea, and all that is in them, but he rested on the seventh day. Therefore, the Lord blessed the Sabbath day and made it holy.*'

The word Sabbath finds its roots right back at the very beginning of our world in Genesis chapter 2 when God rested on the seventh day from His work of creation. The root of the

Sabbath is rest. God stopped. So to a people who have only known the restless, performance-driven culture of Egypt, where their identity was in their ability to achieve - where they were surrounded by a society spurred on by a lust for power, control and influence, a loving God says 'my children stop. For a whole day!'

The Sabbath is good news. Very good news.

But this rest, this stopping, is more than a great idea by God, Sabbath is meant to say something powerful about God Himself! God, as we see in creation, isn't a deity wringing his sweaty hands in panic, trying to milk dry every last drop out of what's there. *No.* He speaks and it comes to be, out of nothing, and he does it in six days, resting on the seventh day just because he can.

He wants us to know, right from the start and in the rhythms of our lives, that He doesn't need anything. He is the one who works, in perfect precision, neither too little nor too much, and we exist to bask in His glory, not barter for its increase.

Isaiah chapter 30:15 declares: *'In repentance and rest is your salvation.'*

Against our backdrop of anxiety, fear, control and busyness Sabbath breaks in and testifies to the world that we don't need anything, because He is everything. And this command was serious. God is God! He does not make suggestions:

'Observe the Sabbath, because it is holy to you. Anyone who desecrates it is to be put to death; those who do any work on that day must be cut off from their people.' (Exodus 31:14)

That's a bit heavy - a bit legalistic and harsh isn't it? Why so hard Lord? In the previous verse, God tells us why: *'You must observe my Sabbaths. This will be a sign between me and you for the generations to come, so you may know that I am the Lord, who makes you holy.'*

Sabbath is a billboard to relationship and salvation in God.

It's a sign pointing people to a creator God who loves them and can transform their lives! Wow. Our communities and future generations can see what Jesus is like and potentially know Him just through me getting this rest. Father wants his people free, and it would seem that rest is a vital pivot between you and I living in Him or tipping back into the ways of the world - into slavery. That's why the punishment is so harsh.

Today?

But what does that mean for us? Should we cease from shopping on Sundays? Does the key to living well and being a witness to our world depend on my approach to one day in seven? Maybe, or maybe not, but let's scoot forward from Mount Sinai, from smoke and trumpets to a field of grain in Galilee.

'At that time Jesus went through the grain fields on the Sabbath. His disciples were hungry and began to pick some heads of grain and eat them. When the Pharisees saw this, they said to him, "Look! Your disciples are doing what is unlawful on the Sabbath." He answered, "Haven't you read what David did when he and his companions were hungry? He entered the house of God, and he and his companions ate the consecrated bread—which was not lawful for them to do, but only for the priests. Or haven't you read in the Law that the priests on Sabbath duty in the temple desecrate the Sabbath and yet are innocent? I tell you that something greater than the temple is here. If you had known what these words mean, 'I desire mercy, not sacrifice,' you would not have condemned the innocent. For the Son of Man is Lord of the Sabbath.' (Matthew 12:1-8)

So here on a farm 1400 years later we discover what man has done with the law. You see the Israelites never quite got it, and by this time, despite a lot of passion and dedication, they had missed the point completely. As we see through the Prophets, God's people lost the promise, they failed to live up to their end of the Covenant and ultimately were invaded and ended up back in captivity. Again, God miraculously restored them, this time through Ezra and Nehemiah, and to avoid such horrors in the future they commit to the Law like never before and tragically miss the point.

You see God always works inside out, heart then action, just like the Ten Commandments, but the Jews tried action first and ended with hearts far from God. They recognised they had broken the contract, disobeyed God and hadn't kept the law. The answer they embraced, which would make any westerner proud, was organisation!

They said 'We will, fuelled by safety first, try and organise our security and identity in God'. Sound familiar?

So, the Jews said 'Let's make other laws to define the law so we have no chance of ever breaking God's commands again.' Seems reasonable. So they asked themselves 'If we are to cease from work on the Sabbath, what is work?' Some clever types began classifying like an eager botanist and stated that for example 'To carry a burden on the Sabbath was work.' But then the inevitable question is 'What is a burden?' You can see where this is going. So, being very technical and leaving no chance for a mistake, the Scribal Law defines a burden as 'Food equal in weight to a dried fig, enough wine for mixing in a goblet, milk enough for one swallow, honey enough to put on a wound, water enough to moisten an eye salve, paper enough to write a customs house notice upon, ink enough to write two letters of the alphabet, reed enough to make a pen,' and so forth. And people say religion makes God boring!?

The God of freedom who spoke Sabbath as a means of living out that freedom, watches it becoming a mess of cruel triviality and controlling legalism.

So, there amongst the crops, this accusation that the disciples are breaking God's law comes at Jesus, and Christ reveals something important. How Sabbath is expressed is dependent upon who is present.

David could eat what was deemed unlawful because he was God's anointed, he was the man chosen to lead the people. God's plan of redemption was at stake, and we see the Sabbath was made for man. The priests were innocent in desecrating the Sabbath because the temple was a visible representation of God and the worship of Him. God's plan came first, the worship of God came first. And now one greater than David and the temple is present! He is Lord of the Sabbath. He gets to choose what Sabbath looks like.

So how does Sabbath now look in light of His presence?

'For in Christ all the fullness of the Deity lives in bodily form, and in Christ you have been brought to fullness. He is the head over every power and authority. In him you were also circumcised with a circumcision not performed by human hands. Your whole self-ruled by the flesh was put off when you were circumcised by Christ, having been buried with him in baptism, in which you were also raised with him through your faith in the working of God, who raised him from the dead.*

When you were dead in your sins and in the uncircumcision of your flesh, God made you alive with Christ. He forgave us all our sins, having cancelled the charge of our legal indebtedness, which stood against us and condemned us; he has taken it away, nailing it to the cross. And having disarmed the powers and authorities, he made a public spectacle of them, triumphing over them by the cross. Therefore, do not let anyone judge you by what you eat or drink, or with regard to a religious festival, a New Moon celebration or a Sabbath day. These are a shadow of the things that were to come; the reality, however, is found in Christ.' (Colossians 2:9-17)

The law was a shadow. Like an outline. It showed us something of what it was to walk with God, and Jesus came and coloured it in! The issue is not what laws we should or shouldn't keep. The issue is, with the law being a shadow, what is it the shadow of?

Jesus. Sabbath was a shadow of Jesus. He is Sabbath; Sabbath looks like Jesus.

'Come to me, all you who are weary and burdened, and I will give you rest. Take my yoke upon you and learn from me, for I am gentle and humble in heart, and you will find rest for your souls. For my yoke is easy and my burden is light.' (Matthew 11:28)

This is even better news than that heard by the refugees in the desert. This is a salvation that is future and a salvation that is present. The invitation to no longer be in control, never worry again, have no fear, do everything from an inexhaustible supply of life, and whatever circumstances you find yourself in be filled with such peace it scares people!

24/7

So, the goal, the command is not one day in seven but a whole lifestyle of carrying Sabbath everywhere we go and letting the rest, that is the finished work of Christ, impact everything we do. Wow! As Hebrews chapter 4:1 declares, the promise is rest. Every part of my life flooded in Him. Rest means always having time for what Jesus is doing. Rest means I am still and always know He is God and can always hear His voice. Rest means my life, success and fruitfulness isn't dependent upon me.

That sounds great. But in practice I have struggled to live anything close to that for most of my life. Life as a Christian has been just as full, stressful, busy and demanding as before Jesus, and I don't think it's just me. I don't seem to come across a lot of rest filled Christians. I rarely ask someone how their week has been and they reply 'well-paced, full of worship, had exactly the right amount of time with Jesus and found the strength to face every challenge overflowing with grace.'

A Facebook post by Billy Kennedy in 2019 highlighted to me the depth of this problem. He was commenting on burnout for church leaders and asking some questions. It went viral. Hundreds commented as people shared their experience and grappled with what was the root problem and what could be done. It unearthed something. It shone a light on a massive failing in Christendom and the post ended up becoming an article in Premier Christianity.

(www.premierchristianity.com/Blog/7)

It is heart-breaking and a little frightening to see so many lives, many I have known personally, put on hold or have to step aside from their call altogether due to stress, breakdowns and burnout. If we can't even find rest working for God's people what chance has anyone got?

Living in rest is a lovely idea but our experience is that it largely seems impossible. Western life, despite more money, time off, holidays, leisure activities and medication, is marked by a deadly disease. Busyness. Everyone is busy. This disease threatens to consume Western Society under the mirage of importance, the 'I matter because I am busy.' Life is lived at a thousand miles an hour and if you're not busy it can feel like something is wrong.

Busyness is your life being so full you are running on empty.

Sadly church life too easily replicates the world and we are overwhelmed by a growing list of meetings, emails, phone calls, visits, vision writing/sharing/changing, social media comment and communication, planning meetings, setting up meetings, packing down meetings, organisation and even meetings about other meetings.

You can begin to glimpse why God was so hot on the Sabbath, making it number four on His top ten.

Leadership

I love how God can speak to you in the midst of the normal and the mundane. Saul was traveling to Damascus, Moses was wandering past a bush and Matthew was busy collecting taxes. I was just popping back from the loo (restroom).

It was 2012 and five months into my work for Highworth Community Church (HCC). I was at the aptly named River Camp, an Elim Bible week set in the Cotswolds. As with most UK based summer camps we had experienced lots of rain but wonderfully lots of spiritual rain as well. I was returning from my ablutions, eager to get back to the main tent and the great time of worship, when God said, 'I have set it up for you.' Instantly I was reminded of Matthew chapter 16:18:

> *'On this rock I will build my church, and the gates of Hades will not overcome it.'*

In that short walk down a muddy rise I knew what God was saying. Firstly that I was not to try and work out my leadership. On starting my work for HCC lots of great people (from outside) had given me lots of good advice. 'You must lead the church.' 'You have to form your own team.' 'Don't let anyone put Saul's armour on you (which took a little explanation),' and 'You need to cast a clear vision and stick to it.'

All advice that had worked in other places and at other times. It can be hard leading in this age when there are so many differing ideas and experiences and where we can be easily enticed to do what has been transformative somewhere else. I just felt to wash people's feet and go with whatever happened, trusting that Jesus would build it, but that seemed a little trite and it was easy to be overwhelmed with all the things I 'should' be doing.

That day Jesus promised me that He would build the Church. Not me, Him. That if I trusted and let go of trying to control then I could live in rest and know that He had set it up for me to let Him build if I would just serve.

Living in rest would be crucial. I knew I had to live in this promise but my attempts flitted from trust to worry. I was inconsistent in doing life from an inner 'Rest for my soul' (Matthew 11:29). Trust flows from rest. Trust knows that God is in charge and is working out His purposes and that He's got you and it saves you from trying to work it all out, sort it all out or hold it all together. This then breeds faith. If it's not dependent on me, then it's dependent on God and living with that realisation is living by faith. And that is what we are all called to, to faith.

After a few years of trial and varying success at a lifestyle of rest I was desperate to find a new way of walking out this rest, trust, faith life. I was keenly aware that it wouldn't take much to tip me over the edge and I could easily become another stressed out leader which is hellish for everyone.

The answer was actually very simple and very challenging.

Not a day off

In early 2016, we returned to the UK from three months of 'advancing' in Cambodia. After 12 weeks of seeking God and desiring to return to serving our church with greater passion and wisdom, I had one word. Sabbath. Trusting God, I diligently began to do a spot of study on this subject. I was struck by Graham Cooke, who defined Sabbath as a day when you stop. That the practice of Sabbath was a practice of stopping. To not achieve anything. Not to pray loads or 'further' my Christian walk but to just stop. To cease from 'work,' to just be.

Sabbath is a day when you don't do anything!

God said 'Stop,' so every week on returning home I set a day, Friday worked for us, and tried to just stop. The thought in my head for what this would feel like, was that feeling you get the second week of a great summer break. You know, where your body suddenly catches up with you, you sleep easier, want to take siestas and your capacity to eat skyrockets. It's that point you hit when you can just sit there, not a thought in your mind, when you know you are utterly content.

Stopping is to be fully present, neither recovering from the past nor straining towards the future. That was the feeling, the inner stillness I felt God was after.

Now this was not a day off. A day off is society's God emptied version of a Sabbath day, a day in my experience (and others I observe) that's a chance to get everything done that we couldn't squeeze into the rest of the week.

But neither was it some rigid set apart day where I couldn't possibly be contacted, and any sniff of work allowed to waft in. Sabbath is about freedom. There are still Fridays where stuff happens, people interrupt, or problems arise. I have learnt to be soft, embrace and retreat, like the waves on the shore.

At first having no plan, ignoring things that 'needed' doing and 'just being' was hard. It felt like a waste and pointless. But slowly I found myself really stopping, really embracing rest and very soon it spilled over into the rest of my week. I found I reacted less. I discovered I could cope with so much more. I found worship easier and more instant.

Life had not magically become simpler. I didn't defer responsibilities or take my foot off the pedal. There is actually far more on my plate now than there was before, but Sabbath enabled me to live free within all this, to work hard without life being hard work, to hold everything God has called me too, gently and lightly.

Disciplines

New Testament Sabbath is the promise of your whole life lived from rest. But the doorway and the fuel for this 24/7 promise I believe is a Sabbath day. Freed from legalistic observance, Sabbath day becomes a spiritual discipline. Like a quiet time or reading the Bible.

Spiritual disciplines are doing what we can, in order to receive the power to do what we cannot.

So, to define Sabbath in the new covenant, I believe, means to practice, 'in freedom', the spiritual discipline of stopping, believing for my every day to be lived in the rest of salvation. Sabbath day is teaching me I am not alone. Everything doesn't depend on me. Things don't have to happen my way. God is with me, helping me and working all things together for my good, so I can be happy no matter what!

Recently, I shocked a member of another church as we were washing up after a joint outreach event. 'I imagine you must be so busy,' she stated, knowing what I do for a job. 'No, I have lots to do but I am never busy.' I may as well have been speaking in Swahili. I could see on her face that like so many, we expect life to be busy, especially if we hold some perceived vital role, and we all passively suffer the consequences.

I have made an active decision to never have a full diary and to always put people first. I don't know if you have ever stood patiently waiting to speak to a leader after a church meeting only to have them blank you as they rushed off to try and pin down something or someone else on their to-do list. I have stood on both sides of that experience in the past and I don't want to be that person.

The discipline of Sabbath helps me keep people first.

People need time and time is a gift but one I have often spent ineffectively. One of the blessings of eternity will be that we'll have so much to do, experience, see and enjoy with all the time we need to do it in! But this life is time limited and therefore this time is an incredible gift. A gift to be enjoyed and a gift to be given. This life is defined by time, driven by time and sadly so often a waste of time. You and I have only a certain number of minutes and hours, and we have no guarantee of when they will end. What we do therefore with this gift, and who we are in the moments of this gift is therefore everything. Paradoxically, stopping and doing nothing with some moments of your time enables you to make more of the time you have. Sabbath is improving my spending.

Time becomes the vital connection between absolute truth and the experience of that truth.

For example, with the temple curtain torn and the Holy Spirit poured out at Pentecost, as a Christian I live every moment of every day filled with God. It's true, irrespective of whether I feel it, experience it or walk in the fullness of it. But unless I commit time to practice entering with boldness the holiest place (Hebrews 10:19) the wonder of the presence of God remains unreleased. It's true, but not true in my every moment. Time enables me to live more and more in that truth, to bring my everyday into the reality of a God who walks with me.

So I practise His presence (see Kathryn's reflection). If I am standing in a queue (line), waiting at the traffic lights or walking to a meeting I put out my hands and simply wait, even for 30 seconds, in His presence.

Three effects of Sabbath parenting

Firstly, and most importantly, living in a greater sense of rest, stopping regularly and constantly rejecting busyness (it easily creeps back in) gives you a greater chance of being the person and the parent you want to be. Parenting, like any leadership position, is hard because so much of the perceived 'success' is in others' hands. You can be the best pastor on the planet but if those you serve don't make good choices, respond to the voice of God and commit to grow, nothing much happens. But you have the power to change you. Being the best you as you serve, irrespective of the results, is the goal. Sabbath means I am more able to live in the moment, more true to who I really am.

Secondly, it gives space and breaks the cycle of busyness. Psychologists have been telling us for years about the vital life defining importance of our early years. It's staggering how we are shaped for good or ill by our formative years. Anyone who has been involved in counselling, prayer ministry or pastoral work knows how the vast majority of the time a person's problems, issues or wounds find their root in childhood experience.

Children need time more than anyone, to develop and discover who they are and how they want to live. Life can so easily be confusing, and this internet generation has so much information to process. They need time to do it at their pace, time to think. Unfortunately, modern family life doesn't allow for any time. Busyness rules the day. Many children's lives are packed tight with a never-ending cycle of school, after school clubs, homework, friends, other clubs and then back to school. A parent becomes an unpaid PA, their role to get said child to said destination on time with the correct equipment or chivvy them through their current task so they can move on to the next.

Embracing Sabbath and actively rejecting busyness has had to look like a reordering of what we do with our time. We can plan not to be busy. And here is where you need to be radical. What are you responsible to God for? What is God asking you to do? What local church are you called to be a part of and how does God want you to love and encourage your fellow believers? Making these your priority means everything else must come second and if it interferes or saps you of time and energy then you have to be radical and let go of them.

This can be really hard. Along with my wife, my brother is my best friend. He leads a great church in Essex and despite sharing blood, love and the same calling I rarely get to see him. It's not because I don't love and value him but that I love and value God more and want to live for what He has put into my hands and stay in rest.

I appreciate this sounds harsh and you prioritising time will look different from me. The issue is not doing things or seeing loved ones and friends. The issue is, am I ordering the life I have and the energy I possess in a way that means I can do all things well, that I am not spread too thin and get time to intentionally Sabbath?

For us when our kids were younger, creating space meant only being part of one after school club a week. Home-schooling our children during their secondary years has not been easy but is worth the challenge with the time it has given us together. My job often involves evenings and weekends so guaranteeing we have lunch together most days is an incredible and vital blessing.

We have also prioritised holidays. Planned retreat has been a big part of our last seven years. We so value the promise of rest and recognise the discipline of it. The main thing we plan when looking ahead is a rhythm of retreat. We are in faith for

God to provide for this, and willing to sacrifice other things (like buying a house) in order to get what we believe is vital space and time to be.

Thirdly, Sabbath reduces arguments. Surely that single fact is enough to motivate most parents! There are passionate people in our household. We are not laid back or passive accepters, we hold opinions and see things differently, but living in rest and the gift of time means these 'flash points' are rarely conflict points.

A good example popped up recently. My daughter had just started some work experience at a local coffee shop. The couple of hours spent there a week had quickly lost its novelty factor and she was finding the limitations of her age (she can't help in the kitchen for instance) meant she often felt in the way and no longer wished to go.

Now this work experience had taken some time to set up and had come from a conversation with her about what her home schooling could look like. We knew objectively this was a good thing for her, and there was great learning to be had. But she didn't want to go. It was all set up for a classic teenage versus parent conflict. Should we tell her she has to go and then endure a heated argument, you know the old 'You committed to this, so you need to do what you said,' or give in avoiding the difficulties, 'Well it's your choice,' and abandon the opportunity? Neither gives space to learn and grow together.

Instead we talked. We had the time and we spent the time. Through this she felt heard and she heard us. She persevered and God blessed her a couple weeks later with paid employment at the coffee shop.

Time enables us to grapple with the hard things of life. How we cope when we feel in the way or undervalued. How we have confidence to find new ways of being involved, and how to find value even when things are hard. The classic teenage rebuff of a parent's advice or command is the 'You don't understand.' Sadly, this often flows less from ignorance of the facts but a lack of capacity to appreciate your child's perspective, from their shoes. These moments become the best moments. The times we can disciple and draw out good from the difficult. But it needs time.

The Lord is my Shepherd

Psalm 23 is probably the most loved and maybe the most misunderstood Psalm. It often gets boxed in the poetic and lovely category, and we miss this as one of the greatest teachings and declarations on spiritual warfare. It is a picture of what the Christian life can be. Of what it truly should look like, independent from your circumstance, to make Jesus your shepherd. It's a radical walk, counter to the world and its systems and values.

Psalm 23 is rest. For me it describes the Sabbath lifestyle and one that is utterly attainable. We just have to be willing to change, and we can start by just stopping. Sabbath is the ability to work hard, while resting in grace and never being busy, fuelled by the regular discipline of intentional Sabbath days and moments.

The fourth Commandment flows naturally to the fifth. Rest gives me time and energy to understand, process and value one of the most important and misunderstood relationships we ever have. How do we relate well to leaders? Read on.

Reflection on Sabbath

By Kathryn

I am a quick learner. As a teacher I used to thrive on the energy and organisation required to maintain 5 practical music classes of 30 young people a day! I loved keeping the lesson fast paced, moving around amongst the kids on their keyboards solving technical or musical questions, being aware of any undesirable behaviour going on anywhere and even finishing with a tidy classroom! I generally quite enjoy being able to multi-task.

However especially since our 'advance-retreat' in Cambodia in 2015 God has been speaking to me about rest, about slowing down, about doing less to do more. When we were there He gave me the melody to a song based on Psalm 63 which says *'Your love is better than life'* (verse 3). As I sat on the balcony singing that through one day, it began to really sink in.

When I was a teenager living in Bognor Regis with my family, I would take long walks along the beach with Jesus, we would speak together, I would marvel at His love. When I was a student in Winchester I would take time on St Giles' hill to just walk with Jesus, to be alone with Him. But after our children came along things were different. As I'm sure any other parents know, you start to know what tiredness really is! As a young mum I had some beautiful insights and grace from God as He knew my needs, time constraints and taught me to access His presence and peace faster. What I previously gained in a half hour with Jesus I could now feel in a few minutes. He is so good!

But, there is always more. My capacity for His presence increased as we spent hours worshipping in Mozambique but I had always been impacted by a book called *'The Practice of the*

Presence of God' by Brother Lawrence. The idea that I am always at rest in His presence whatever I am doing. I longed for this and over the last few years have tried to pursue it.

I started to do some practical things to help continue to live out Sabbath. As I walked the short distance from our flat to my office I would intentionally slow my pace and match the words 'Be still and know' to its tempo. I would stop myself mid-task (like sorting out the laundry) and fix my thoughts on Him.

Recently as we have experienced the Covid-19 lockdown period God has called to me again to stop. This time to literally learn to do nothing. To sit outside my back door (nicer in the sun) knowing a whole list of things that I could be doing, not even bringing my Bible, journal or worship music and just doing nothing. I am having to practise it, this doing nothing! But you know what? Of course He is speaking to me in the detail of a plant or a roof or a cloud or the wind. I am learning more rest.

My desire is that within me is a great cathedral of His presence. A calm, ornate, elegant space of stillness. A place where His Spirit can dwell. A place so solidly built that it is constantly there no matter what my physical body is doing. It's a work in progress!

Eleven

Honour

*'"Honour your father and mother," which is the first commandment
with a promise.'*

Ephesians 6:2

I was sitting on a United Airlines flight somewhere above the
North Atlantic when the horror of parenthood fully hit me. I
was halfway through a quite brilliant biography on the life of
David Wilkerson, written by his son Gary. David had
impacted my life as a man who, armed only with the gospel,
walked into the gang culture of the 1960's New York, and
without a shred of cultural relevance saw the love of Jesus
change so many lives that it spawned the Teen Challenge
movement (read *The Cross and the Switchblade* to find out
more). He was promoted to glory in 2011 and Gary has written
an inspiring and deeply honest account of his Dad.

And he pulls no punches.

Without criticising or shaming his earthly father, Gary paints
a picture of a man who overcame so many barriers and was
inspired to bring the power of the gospel to thousands, and yet
one who struggled to really grasp that simplest of facts; that
God loved him! Yes, he knew it as a truth. Yes, he could accept
it when things were going well or his ministry was fruitful, but
due in part to a strict performance based Pentecostal

upbringing, when things went wrong or didn't work out he was left unsettled and uncertain of being beloved. We can't hide things like this and despite his best efforts this love deficit affected everything, especially his relationship with Gary. David was tireless, driven and uber committed but Gary struggled to find and know acceptance and value in just being himself, David's son.

> Our own brokenness will always affect the ones we love the most.

I was shocked and deeply challenged. He never got it. He never broke through on a core issue in his life. What about me? I don't want to be a father whose deep unresolved issues affect my children, despite whatever success I have for the Kingdom. The full horror of parenthood hit me. You always fail.

Years ago, I read about how Wesley and Whitfield and other members of the famed Holy Club at Oxford evaluated the success of each day by asking themselves at days end a whole series of questions. They included:

- Do I give the Bible time to speak to me every day?
- Am I enjoying prayer?
- When did I last speak to someone else of my faith?
- Am I proud?
- Is Christ real to me?

It had inspired me to reflect more on each day, to think through the choices I had made (and not made), my relationship with God, the things I had said and how I had treated others. It was all going relatively well until I became a dad. You realise the person you really are when you are trying to calm a crying baby at 3am, who resists every idea and piece of advice you've gleaned from a church full of mums, whilst struggling to recall the last time you slept for more than four hours in a row, and drawing a complete blank as to how you are going to survive the coming day at work.

I thought I was a lovely young Christian man until tiredness, responsibility, worry and zero free time came knocking at my door.

And then they grow up! Suddenly, just as you think 'I've got this,' when you know you can change a nappy one handed and still remain doo doo free. When you feel at one with the rhythms of your baby and understand instinctively what certain cries really mean (tired, hurt, hungry, love deficit, just crying), you can successfully install and secure a baby car seat (don't get me started, all invented by failed Ikea engineers), and you believe you could represent your country at the winding Olympics. Suddenly they are talking, thinking for themselves, asking questions about death, making and losing friends and, worst of all, affected by everything you say and do.

My daily reflections were often filled with all the things I wished I had said and done or regret over some of the things I had said and done. However, it wasn't just my personal perspective of how I was doing as a parent that challenged me, but also the people I have been called to work with and work for.

Escaping the past

I have always loved deep conversations and discovering what I and others are really thinking and feeling. I can remember my poor father suffering as my mother and I (we are wired the same) went hammer and tongs late into the night on some God subject, while he tried to find a moment's pause in the debate to fall asleep or finish a chapter of the latest John Grisham novel!

The more time I have spent with people, really listening and trying to ask good questions, the more I have realised the huge negative impact our past can have on every one of us. We are products of our past, our imperfect response to, and our way of trying to deal with, pain.

I guess it is a result of 'the fall' that we are more affected and shaped by the bad and the painful moments in life. So many of us have sadly just learned to either cope with these core areas of brokenness, hoping they stay hidden, or bury them so deep we are shamefully unaware they exist.

As a child of very keen gardeners, summer chores invariably involved weeding the garden. Unlike my brother, I was always keen to get my 'to do list' completed as quickly as possible, and discovered that digging up a weed, especially when the ground is dry, takes time. It is far simpler to snap what you can see off and in no time at all my flower border of responsibility looked rather nice. Job done?

So often our form of Christianity acts like a lazy weeding session. When a 'weed' breaks through the surface we try a quick prayer, ministry time, meditation or repeat a positive Bible verse, snap off the leaves and think everything is okay. But we discover the weeds quickly return. Maybe it's anger or worry, depressive thoughts, a hatred of self, an under valuing of others, fear of loneliness or of poverty, feelings of inferiority, inability to forgive, or something or someone that really easily winds us up. These things have roots and if we want the fullness of the cross to impact us, we need to do a bit of digging.

This has all stirred a great desire in me to see myself and others really set free from these things, and I am thankful for excellent teaching from the likes of the Plumbline Course, Freedom in Christ and Restoring the Foundations, as well as a host of mentors and teachers equipping me and opening my eyes.

Problem is, the more my eyes have been opened to the bad roots in our lives, the more I was confronted with the uncomfortable truth that a frightening majority of them were rooted in our experience of being parented (or not). Whether present or absent, parental figures affect every one of us at the deepest level.

I have occasionally imagined, with a sinking heart, one of our children years from now being asked to make themselves comfortable on a plush official looking couch and then asked the classic counselling question:

'Now tell me about your father?'

I am imperfect and this imperfection is not neutral. The people I love most in the whole universe are the ones most harmed by my lack, my brokenness, my unhealed past and unresolved hurts. This is the horror. This is the failure.

Like an addict in recovery this denial must be overcome. Sorry if that's a bit depressing or negative but without embracing this fact change will always be superficial and limited.

So back to the plane and we are slightly further across the North Atlantic.

Scarily, I was actually very aware of one of my deepest issues. A few years ago I had been at a conference with a lady called Dawna de Silva, and we were doing a group exercise with about 500 of us! She got us to close our eyes, asked the Holy Spirit to come, and then began to ask us some questions, the idea being we weren't to give the 'right,' 'Christian' answers, but the ones we really believed, our personal truth. We got to 'How does Father God see you' and I was shocked when the word DISAPPOINTED blazed into my mind.

Now I have been in and around Church my whole life, I knew God really didn't feel that about me and yet deep down that was my default position. The truth was head not heart knowledge. So many Christians are caught in this trap. We know objectively for example that God loves us and can even quote verses to prove it, but this knowledge is of no real use to us because we haven't experienced it and let it shape who we are.

I believed and lived in the truths that God accepted me. He had forgiven me, loved me and was always there for me. I knew He was there to pick me up, but I didn't know He was there to back me up. I struggled to accept He was proud of me, that He was pleased with who I am.

God's pleasure in us is foundational to our identity. God the Father only uttered a few audible words about His Son during His 33 years on the planet. He could have said so many things, but He focused on affirmation and identity. *'This is my Son, whom I love, with Him I am well pleased'* (Matthew 3:17). This was at His baptism before He did any ministry, miracles or mankind-saving-suffering. The Father valued Him for who He was. Loved Him for who He was, and was pleased, was proud of Him for who He was.

And this matters.

Changing the past

I recognised something in those moments (at 30,000 feet) of how that affected me. How, a bit like David Wilkerson, I was lost when things went wrong, my Christian walk looking like a seismograph during a particularly violent quake, all peaks and troughs. I felt like I was never going to cut it or be the man God had made me to become. I was never doing as well as I should, and thus as I looked ahead, I almost expected to fail. Not good.

I was in one of those raw wonder moments. They hurt, but you know if you allow the Holy Spirit to work, they will be massively redemptive. 'Jesus what do I do?' 'How do I enable my children to live in and out from the good aspects of my parenting and not the bad?' 'How do I get free and not see myself as a disappointment to you'?

Unfortunately the answer wasn't to bury my head ostrich style. But it was easy. Humble yourself.

Okay. Easy but scary and painful. For me this looked like two things: repentance and healing, which I guess should always be together.

Firstly, repentance. A couple of days later, as we had settled into a week's mission at the amazing, We Will Go Ministries in Jackson Mississippi, I gathered the children one morning and asked for their forgiveness. I shared my experience on the plane and some specific areas I knew I often messed up in as a dad. Most of all I asked them to forgive my brokenness, for all the times I wasn't leading by example, hungering after God, or letting prayer shape my day. True repentance to others should always be hard because if done humbly, it should not demand or control the right response. My children didn't have to forgive me, and I could only offer them room to do so. It was a blessing however that they did, and we shared some precious moments hugging and praying.

Secondly, healing. I knew to see this change would take more than post-it note Bible verses on the bathroom mirror or getting someone to pray for me at the end of a meeting. It would take a deep encounter with God to shift this lie and enable me to be free. I get prayed for at the end of meetings and it's always great. We often have Bible verses on our bathroom mirror, in front of the loo or by the kettle and it encourages me. Both these, and other tools besides, are great ways of focusing on God and walking out the truths. However, shifting deep rooted issues that have been part of our thinking, lifestyle and world view for years often takes intentional time and a profound encounter.

God is so kind. He never diagnoses without providing the treatment. After our week serving in downtown Jackson, we were off to Bethel Church in Redding, California. It's a church that has impacted my life brilliantly in many ways, and we now had the chance to visit because great missionary friends of ours were studying there. One of the ministries they run is called Sozo (Greek for salvation) a healing ministry that aims: 'To get to the root of those things hindering your personal connection with God - Father, Son and Holy Spirit.' It sounded perfect and due to the wonders of technology I was able to book in online.

My two-hour session with Bethel Sozo was so good. I was cared for and honoured without being cajoled or forced into anything. They allowed the intentional space for me to let Holy Spirit speak and bring the healing He wanted to. I met with God beautifully and simply. The root was gently pulled up and I sat there, tears rolling down my cheeks, overcome with how my heavenly Father really felt about me.

'He thinks I am great!' 'He is proud of me!'

This encounter changed me, but, like any God thing, I still have to choose to live in the freedom and truth of it and that's where post-it notes or prayer times can be really helpful.

A quick word of advice. You don't have to go to Bethel or anywhere else to meet Jesus in a life changing way but sometimes it helps. God sees your heart, and as we see with Jesus in the Gospels, He is always willing to heal and transform those who genuinely seek after Him. Therefore be at peace that it is not about the package, minister or latest idea but humbly allowing others to lead you to the Cross. There are good ministries out there that can serve you brilliantly if you want to change but always take advice from those you respect and who love you before diving in.

Our parents

So, repentance and healing. Two solutions to aid my parenting imperfection. I recognised my failings and also that I am not just a parent, but like every one of us, I am someone who has been parented. What does my 'epiphany on the plane' mean for my mum and dad? If I am to be free, how do I respond as a child?

I have great parents who I count as my friends and love doing the Kingdom of God with. I grew up feeling loved and accepted. I wasn't beaten or neglected. My parents had an active and living faith in Jesus Christ and worked hard at the things that were important to God. We went on some nice holidays (despite the rain) and I never went hungry. Admitting I was imperfect was one thing but labelling them the same seemed judgemental and unbiblical. For starters what about the fifth commandment to *'honour your father and mother'* (Exodus 20:12). How can I cast a critical eye their way?

A slightly strange episode in the book of Genesis about Noah's life has taught me more than the far more famous world shaping story found a few chapters earlier. Yes, a story of drunkenness, exposure, humiliation and reverence has impacted me more than the crazy faith and obedience of the Ark and all that followed; call me weird! In Genesis chapter 9, after all the cool, dove, olive branch, land appearing again and the first rainbow stuff we read:

'Noah, a man of the soil, proceeded to plant a vineyard. When he drank some of its wine, he became drunk and lay uncovered inside his tent. Ham, the father of Canaan, saw his father naked and told his

two brothers outside. But Shem and Japheth took a garment and laid it across their shoulders; then they walked in backward and covered their father's naked body. Their faces were turned the other way so that they would not see their father naked.' (vs 20-23)

So probably due to a lack of any decent brew for the last couple of years he rather underestimates his limits and the story unfolds acting like a government warning on the dangers of alcohol as Noah gets drunk, strips off and passes out in public. The youngest of Noah's sons, Ham (who would later go on to invent a perfect sandwich filling), saw his Father's failure and went and told his brothers who covered up poor dad without looking, using a clever backwards robe between the shoulders manoeuvre.

So that's that. Noah, despite being a man of great faith, and like many such men who would come after him, has his flaws and vices. But surprisingly this story isn't a cautionary tale on Noah but Ham. Dad wakes up, finds out what had happened and curses Ham's bloodline! What is going on?

Our Leaders

And let's push things slightly further. Leadership in the church at all levels is about being a spiritual mum and dad. We may find it a little dicey to critique our parents, but what about our leaders? We live in a culture that positively delights in revealing leadership failures. How do we process the role of people who have influence and input into our lives, who will not get everything right or be dealing with their own brokenness and weakness?

I was privileged during my first couple of years in leadership to be a part of the C.net weekly leaders gathering in Southampton on a Tuesday morning. Here I got to spend a couple of hours every week with some of my heroes. These were the leading lights of the church stream I was a part of, many of whom had already had a major impact upon my life. Basically, it was a feedback time and a prayer time, and I learnt so much. I was allowed into these people's lives as they shared honestly and openly, which was wonderful and also challenging. Suddenly, I became very aware of these people's flaws, struggles and weaknesses. Like Dorothy in the Wizard of Oz, I was allowed to see 'behind the curtain' and it floored me. Like Ham I saw their nakedness, not literally, but emotionally and spiritually. These people were not perfect. Like me, these people still needed to grow and be changed and some were even unaware of some of their own needs. What was I to do?

Now these people's imperfections were not failures like Noah's, but the principle still applies. Like Ham I wanted to point these things out and tell others, but that was when the power of this story really hit me. You see what Ham did made sense in our 'transparency' culture. Noah had failed. He was drunk and he was naked. Ham was justified in his actions and made sure others knew about it. He added to the situation, magnified his father's failure and heaped upon it more shame. It's what we see happening in the media every day. How many lives have been ruined and devastated by an overeager journalist who leans heavily upon people's 'right to know'? How often has this been repeated in the church with leaders' failures publicly exposed?

Let's burst a cultural bubble right here. No one else has a 'right' to know another's failure or mess, however public that person might be. The Cross gives everyone a 'right' to redemption. Walking in the light is not permission to expose but permission to heal and restore.

As Sharon Hodde Miller identifies:

'There is certainly a time for light. But there is also a time for covering. Covering is different from hiding. Covering comes after the sin has come to light, and this distinction matters.'

(www.sheworshiops.com)

Now, please hear me, I am not endorsing a cover up. If a person has broken the law then we need to involve the proper authorities. This is not about pretending something hasn't happened or not dealing biblically with sin. This is about honour. We do not honour our parents or leaders because they are perfect, we honour them because this provides a culture of restoration. Shem and Japheth did not hide Noah's shame, they covered it. They didn't treat him as he was in that dark moment but as who they knew he could be.

Changing your future

And so, we are called, like Shem and Japheth, to cover over another's nakedness. Similar to my response to my children we do this in two ways. Forgiveness and healing.

Firstly, forgiveness. I could easily write a whole book, or maybe a whole series of books on this. It is THE most important thing we do. When the disciples asked Jesus to teach them how to pray in Luke 11, Jesus said at least a quarter of your prayer life should be about forgiveness! (look again at the Lord's Prayer).

Forgiveness can feel impossible or unfair but is not about letting someone else off the hook, rather letting yourself off the hook. Unforgiveness is a horrid beast that acts like a poison affecting and infecting our lives. It will become a barrier between deep relationships with the people you love and with God. Mark 11:25 says *'Whenever you stand praying, forgive'* (NASB). Forgiveness is commanded and expected not because Jesus is demanding but because He knows how destructive it will be if you don't.

Forgiveness is a command of pure love.

The great news is Jesus never commands something without provision. He himself, through the Holy Spirit, will provide what you need to be obedient. Forgiveness therefore is a grace empowered choice. We choose it and the Holy Spirit gives us the power to do it.

This was wonderfully fulfilled in the life of Corrie Ten-Boom. She and her sister Betsie had been imprisoned in Ravensbrook Concentration Camp by the Nazis during World War II, after they were found to be complicit in rescuing Jews. Her sister died in that utterly God-forsaken place. A few years later, Corrie was confronted by one of her former prison guards who asked for her forgiveness. In her own words:

'And I stood there, I whose sins had again and again to be forgiven and could not forgive. Betsie had died in that place - could he erase her slow terrible death simply for the asking?

"I wrestled with the most difficult thing I had ever had to do. For I had to do it — I knew that. The message that God forgives has a prior condition: that we forgive those who have injured us."

Forgiveness is an act of the will, not an emotion. "Jesus, help me!" I prayed. "I can lift my hand. I can do that much. You supply the feeling."

So I thrust out my hand.

And as I did, an incredible thing took place. The current started in my shoulder, raced down my arm, sprang into our joined hands. And then this healing warmth seemed to flood my whole being, bringing tears to my eyes.

"I forgive you, brother!" I cried. "With all my heart."

For a long moment we grasped each other's hands, the former guard and the former prisoner. I had never known God's love so intensely as I did then.'   (Tramp for the Lord, Hodder & Stoughton 1975)

Forgiveness is possible.

Secondly, healing. On a recent holiday I was slightly recklessly navigating a small rapids section of the Ardeche river in France and smashed my leg on a rock. Now I have injured, bruised and cut my legs many times before, so it was no shock when a large lump, dark bruise and red blood appeared. Every time I have hurt my physical body I have needed healing. If this is true for our physical bodies, how much more for my spirit and emotions! We are so quick to respond to physical hurts, which often can 'naturally' heal themselves, yet slow or just plain irresponsible when we come to emotional and spiritual hurts, which generally do not naturally heal and have far more devastating consequences. This type of healing needs the Holy Spirit. It needs you to be open and sharing with those you trust. It needs a commitment.

The good news is you tend to get more than you bargained for. When I am able to let God heal me, He doesn't just put me back the way I was but always adds something else. I come out the other side stronger, closer to Jesus and closer to people.

The healed bring healing

This work, choosing redemption rather than punishment, has its outworking in all our relationships, especially when our children mess up.

A couple of years ago, Kathryn and I were enjoying a night away in Windsor. We were sitting outside the famous castle sunning ourselves on a bench, having just enjoyed a lovely lunch, when my phone rang. It was one of our children sheepishly calling to inform us that they had been looking at some stuff on their phone that they shouldn't have, but in doing so had got infected by a virus (the phone and not them). They had been busted and were phoning to head off the situation. I managed to stop myself from going all out and quickly embraced the three steps to not making the situation worse:

1. Big pause
2. Let go of anger and or fear
3. Respond with grace

I assured them that we loved them. That it would all be ok. Prayed for them over the phone and talked through how they could process their mess with Jesus.

God's answer to sin is not punishment but grace. Why would my answer be any different? We don't need to be a theological wizard to know the Old Covenant didn't work because no law or punishment can change the heart.

Honour means to 'give weight to' (the word means heavy, weighty). We honour God by giving Him 'weight', significance and value in our lives. When it comes to people though, we recognise they are imperfect and therefore honour is not a blanket acceptance of who a person is. I don't honour my parents by glossing over their imperfections. Honour is recognising and valuing the good someone has brought into our lives. Honour acts like a surgeon's knife, separating the positive from the negative. Honour should be a baton exchange for righteousness and a roadblock to sin.

I honour my mum and dad by fully allowing the good of their lives to be reflected in me and the bad to be forever left by the roadside.

Life has often been likened to a great relay race, each generation passing on to the next. Imagine if we ever got this.

- Imagine if each generation was able to truly *'hold on to what is good,* (and) *reject every kind of evil.'* (1 Thessalonians 5:21-22)
- Imagine if each person's pain and brokenness wasn't carried forward
- Imagine if sin's effects always ended with us
- Imagine if every hard-fought revelation and truth was faithfully grasped and held onto by those who came after
- Imagine the church we would be today if every generation had practised this honour

Honour is the ability to receive from and serve parents and leaders, discerning and leaving any mess, embracing the good and carrying it forward in our lives. Can you honour your parents and leaders? Can you commit to your own process of repentance, forgiveness and healing, that this great baton exchange would be true in your life?

To do so takes a radical understanding and a godly embracing of something we all suffer from, live under and despite our best efforts, learn to live with in both ourselves and others. Read on.

Reflection on Honour
By Caleb

In that one moment, in a room, on the base in Jackson Mississippi, America, I saw my dad, whom I've spent my life growing up with and who had always been there for me, lay down any pride of being secure and having it all together. Of appearing like the hero that we all see our dads as growing up, and humbling himself and admitting he's made mistakes and he hasn't always had it worked out.

I remember feeling in the moment quite surprised, a bit worried, maybe shocked but actually after that day didn't really think about it that much, and didn't really worry about it. What's done is done, as they say, and it can't be changed, I can just change what I do about it. My dad asked for forgiveness and I and my siblings accepted with hugs and prayers, but I wasn't terribly shocked or had my whole world shaken because I was used to mum and dad being honest. Honest about their feelings and troubles and what our situation was, it probably saved me from doubt, the fact that they hadn't tried to create a false image of 'everything's fine'.

I find that seeing the mistakes and flaws of someone you have always looked up to and idolised hard sometimes, just like is said in this chapter, but what I found after this moment is that from a place of forgiving and accepting I could come to respect and admire my father even more than I did before, because he was prepared to be honest and truthful within any mistakes he had made.

I confess I don't always remember to honour my Father and Mother, if it's honouring daily or just through how I act, and maybe get a little annoyed sometimes. But that's why I think honour must be a daily endeavour, with my respect for them going hand in hand with my acceptance and forgiveness of them that leads me on to '... honour my mum and dad by fully allowing the good of their lives to be reflected in me and the bad to be forever left by the roadside.'

Twelve

Weakness

'But we have this treasure in jars of clay to show that this all-surpassing power is from God and not from us.'

2 Corinthians 4:7

He stood awkwardly upon his crutches, repeating the request to the confused shop assistant.

'I would like a new pair of shoes.'

A simple and very normal request in a shoe shop - if you had any feet that is. 'I am sorry sir but there is nothing I can do for you,' the assistant replied in a caring but firm manner. The man, a church curate, hesitated and then with fresh confidence said, 'It's okay, I would like a pair of black shoes in a size eight.'

Upon returning, the assistant reluctantly but gently placed a leg stump into one of the shoes, the power of God came down and instantly a new leg and foot formed. The same thing happened to the other leg and the curate left gingerly walking out with new shoes and new feet praising God!

The night before, he had been taking supper with a guy called Smith Wigglesworth. The subject came up of his amputation, and the difficulty artificial limbs had in those days (early 20th

Century), when Smith had suddenly declared to him 'in the morning go and buy a new pair of shoes!' Thinking he was a victim of a cruel joke he retired to his room where God spoke to him. 'Do as my servant commanded!'

I remember first reading this well documented story when I was 21. My brother had passed onto me a biography of this Wigglesworth guy which so far had been chock full of these incredible stories of faith and the power of God.

They were wonderful. And I was really quite annoyed. Cross even. 'Why was it so easy for this guy?' This ex-plumber was just seeing crazy things happening and walking in the promises of Christ like it was the easiest thing ever, like falling off a log (as we would say in the UK). He was like a real King Midas, everything he touched turned to gold or miracles in Smith's case, and it made my own struggles in prayer and reaching out look like embarrassing failures.

I almost stopped reading I was so disheartened.

It was then I turned to a chapter about Polly, and with tears in my eyes I repented of my sin and something clicked. Polly was Wigglesworth's beloved wife, his teammate and best friend. It was her who actually pulled him into the Baptism in the Holy Spirit, into preaching, and into miracles. She died suddenly in 1913 when they were both still young before their ministry had truly begun. His children confessed years later of how this broke their father's heart and that they would often find him weeping over her loss.

Smith Wigglesworth did 'the stuff' as John Wimber would say. Travelled the world, made it his goal to daily lead someone personally to Christ, preached to thousands and saw the miraculous power of God break out in hundreds of lives (he is reported to have seen 14 people raised from the dead), and he did all this, mourning the loss of his love. Suddenly I didn't see a superstar or someone for whom everything just seemed to happen. I saw a brave, broken man putting Jesus first. I saw a weak servant with the willingness to trust in God.

We live in a world where society continues the desperate search for heroes. If you walk the streets of our nation's capital, you see a London littered with monuments and statues to those who past generations elevated (rightly or wrongly), those who shaped our nation for good or ill, like Victoria, Nelson, Churchill and Peter Pan (ok scrub the last one but it is a nice statue). Today our heroes are sports stars, movie stars, pop stars and a whole bunch of other 'famous' people who must be stars of something. Today, more than ever, we exalt gift and ability. Reality shows have made millions discovering hidden talent and you may have come across the acronym GOAT. YouTube is aflame with endless vids on who is the GOAT, the Greatest Of All Time, be it concerning football, basketball or rapping!

Gift. Talent. Ability. Things we easily elevate within church and Christianity to our loss.

I listened to a podcast recently on Rosa Parks. The lady who refused to give up her seat on the bus to a white man and sparked a city-wide protest that went a long way to seeing segregation overturned and equal rights established in the US. She now has a museum built in her honour and you even get a holiday on Rosa Parks day. The podcast reflected that this elevation actually disempowers her message. Her simple courage had now become something so big that she was up there, and we forget that every one of us can make a simple stand against injustice.

Jesus is not looking for heroes! God does not call us because we are gifted. His Kingdom is not built on ability. Talent has no bearing on being fruitful in Christ.

Jars of clay

Most of the events and wisdom in this book I have gleaned from the worst decade of my life. I daily face three major challenges that despite repeated doctor's appointments, specialists and endless reading remain undiagnosed. They are not the worst things anyone has ever faced. I am sure that some of you reading this face challenges that make my struggles look like a teddy bear's picnic. But these are my difficulties and they are the context in which this book has been written.

Every day my back hurts. At night I cannot sleep without applying deep heat cream or the use of a hot water bottle to deaden the pain. I have to live within a fine balance of keeping fit, otherwise it gets worse, and not overdoing it, which also makes it worse. Some days it's just stiff and others it really burns, and everything is more difficult. Bursitis and frozen shoulders come with the territory. My brother has an arthritic condition called Ankylosing Spondylitis. My symptoms are very similar but the major condition, a progressive stiffening of the spine isn't manifest so it remains an undiagnosed inflammation issue.

In 2008 during a particularly stressful time due to huge financial challenges I started not sleeping well. Like some nights I didn't. For over twelve years now, despite the exacerbating issues being resolved, I have really struggled with sleep. For most of this past decade four hours of broken sleep has been a win and sleep tablets have been an unenviable support. My problem is dropping off and I can lie there, totally relaxed knowing everything is in place for sleep to happen, but the final switch doesn't get flicked, something that takes me from rest to lala land fails. I have spent hundreds of nights grappling with whether to carry on trying at 3am to get to sleep naturally or take a sleeping tablet. The tablets generally work but the next day you feel groggy and almost hungover, so it isn't a great option, just a survival one. I have tried ocean sounds, camomile tea, no screens, no caffeine, a glass of wine, no alcohol, melatonin, black out blinds, a new mattress and a dozen different bed regimes.

I totally understand why sleep deprivation is a popular torture technique, with the many dark nights of the soul I have experienced, when all seems lost and I don't want to carry on. Anger and frustration can easily surface, that's something a cracked phone screen can testify to (it was sent flying across the room in one moment of exhausted temper) and the sense of depression when nothing works, or no prayer seems to change things makes you wonder if this is your lot.

And finally, I generally feel awful all the time. Irrespective of whether the previously mentioned challenges are in play, I constantly feel like I am coming down with a heavy cold and that at my best I am running on about 60%. It makes no difference if my back isn't playing up and I have had a better season of sleep. My brain feels foggy and I constantly feel drained and lethargic. Most days are relegated to an exercise in just making it to the end. Despite a barrage of blood tests, on several occasions, and my doctor's continued support at finding a reason for this, it remains an anomaly - there is no reason why I feel like I do. I do not experience the classic boom and bust of Chronic Fatigue Syndrome (one day's action you pay for the next) so it all remains a big question mark.

I have struggled for over a decade with these three things. I have been prayed for by the world and his wife and yet so far, nothing has changed.

The treasure

What great news! No really. The gospel really is good news. The good news is Jesus has done everything for you. Before you were born, he carried all your sin, paid the price for it, died in your place and then was resurrected to a new life, blazing a way into eternity that we can all follow in. And now since you have been born, you can have all of the above just merely by believing in Him and accepting it. You can then welcome Him into your life to keep working and keep bringing the Kingdom of God to earth through your weakness. The good news, the gospel, is Jesus being brilliant - not you - and that He will carry on being brilliant until the day you meet Him face to face and then it will be even more brilliant because:

'He will wipe every tear from their eyes. There will be no more death or mourning or crying or pain, for the old order of things has passed away.' (Revelation 21:4)

And:

'There will be no more night. They will not need the light of a lamp or the light of the sun, for the Lord God will give them light. And they will reign for ever and ever.' (Revelation 22:5)

The good news is God doesn't need your gift, He's not after talented people and a successful life of following Christ is not dependent upon your strength.

My weakness is good news because paradoxically, at least in the world's system, this last decade has been the best of my life. The struggles themselves are not good news (we are not getting into a masochistic faith) but despite them, despite the hardships, I am experiencing the time of my life. I have been more fruitful, had more revelation, seen more lives changed, have been more transformed to be like Christ and experienced more joy and peace than ever before. I have been more obedient, more loving, more worshipful and learnt more about humility in years, which at least on paper, were the worst.

Revelation

My first real experience of this 'Wonder of Weakness' came at an old Victorian farm, now a residential Bible school located in the Scottish Borders about one hour east of Edinburgh, on a hill near a town called Duns. Surrounded by pine forest, Kings Bible School occupied a beautiful spot and was a perfect place for me to grow.

Having recovered from my vestiphobia (look it up) due in part to a year spent in Africa wearing shorts, no shoes and occasionally a T-shirt (think surfer dude without the long hair or wave riding skills), I purchased some shirts and ties and in September 1995 I got on a coach headed for Scotland.

That year's intake was a fantastic cross section of age, status and experience. There were over thirty students, the youngest eighteen, the oldest a pensioner. It included families and their children and students not just from the UK but North America as well. Some were there for a year out, some to 'study' for ministry and others to just simply know God more. They became my family for a year.

From the start I was determined I would be the best I could be and maybe more. I had come to Jesus 15 months before, weary and heavy laden and found the promised rest (Matthew 11:28) but now I felt free and renewed. I was going to make up for the wasted years, I was going to be amazing for Jesus! That first term I threw myself into everything, and tried to be the hardest worker, server, worshipper, listener, friend, and student possible. If someone had asked 'Does anyone here have a great prayer life?' I would have shot my hand in the air. 'Me!' I was cramming every spare moment with prayer and worship, trying, trying, trying to be great for Jesus but I had a problem. The harder I pushed, the further away God seemed, in fact by mid-November I couldn't feel God's presence at all, everything was cold and dry.

Now being at Bible school is the worst possible place to be to not find God. Every day it was in my face and I couldn't escape. Prayers dribbled from my lips; worship was an awful emptiness and the Bible a mass of dead words. I pushed myself, 'I must break through' I thought 'God is testing me,' but the harder I worked the worse it got. I got every lecturer and staff member to pray for me and... nothing! I was ashamed and fearful that I would never know Holy Spirit's presence again (the most precious thing in my life). That Christmas I went home a broken man and dreaded the return to college.

Just as Jesus so tenderly restored Peter after his failure (see John 21), He began to steer me home. His kindness leads us to repentance. Back home my Mum passed me something written by Oswald Chambers:

'If you can stay in the midst of turmoil unperplexed and calm because you see Jesus then that is God's plan for your life. Not that you may be able to say, "I have done this and that and now it's all right". We have an idea that God is leading us to a certain goal, a desired haven. He is not. To God the question of our getting to a particular end is a mere incident. What we call the process, God calls the end. God's purpose is that you can depend on him and his power now. God's purpose is that you see him walking on the waves. No shore in sight. No success. Just the absolute certainty that it is all right because you see Him.' (www.utmost.org)

It hit me like a barn door! I was so desperate to do something for Jesus, be something for Jesus, that I had totally missed Jesus Himself. I had thought to follow Christ I needed to be strong but now I was learning the painful lesson that He was after my weakness.

I remember that January I was down to lead the first worship time since the holiday. I was desperate to share something powerful and moving, but all I could do was sit there and be honest. I felt I was letting people down as I shared my pain at feeling so far from God, that it was like He had stepped back, and I had discovered how powerless I was. At the end Tony the Principal, said 'Well it's good to know Matt is the same as all of us!' Everyone laughed and they were the words I most needed to hear. The Good Shepherd carried me those first few weeks of 1996 like never before. I was set free from a need to perform or attain, and freed to just enjoy the pilgrimage of life following Christ.

When we say God is unstoppable it means my stuff can't stop Him! God doesn't want or need your gifts. He wants you.

Transformed frailty

I know many of you reading this face far bigger challenges than me. This book is not me heroically declaring 'Look what I've done despite my ailments' and 'Don't let your problems stand in the way of your dreams', or even a 'You can do anything.' This book I dearly hope is a spotlight on truth that despite or even because of my weakness, God has still worked, still loved, still turned up and somehow my mess has glorified Him. The good news is you can lead, parent and disciple, whatever personal challenges you face because truly 'greater is He that is in you, than he that is in the world,' (1 John 4:4).

Centuries ago, this guy formerly known as Saul encounters God as he grapples, a little like me, with the mess of the world, and God speaks some utterly stunning words that are in total conflict with how we think life works.

In the second letter to the church at Corinth the Apostle Paul records an insight into his prayer life. He was grappling, as we probably all do, with the things in his life that seemed to hold him back or get in the way of him being all that he could be. He describes a thorn in his flesh, a messenger from Satan, a torment. And like any good disciple he brought it to his God in deep heartfelt prayer:

'Three times I pleaded with the Lord to take it away from me. But he said to me, "My grace is sufficient for you, for my power is made perfect in weakness." Therefore, I will boast all the more gladly about my weaknesses, so that Christ's power may rest on me. That is why, for Christ's sake, I delight in weaknesses, in insults, in hardships, in persecutions, in difficulties. For when I am weak, then I am strong.' (2 Corinthians 12:8-10)

Now commentators have been mystified at what this ailment or torment was, but that's not the issue. The issue is Paul felt he was being held back by something, pleads with God for it to be taken out of the way, and God puts him straight and tells him that weakness accelerates his ministry rather than hinders it. The literal translation is: God's power is perfected in a weakness or ailment that on paper deprives someone from enjoying or accomplishing what they would like to be and do for Jesus. What Paul thought held him back actually enabled him. Paul's struggle was the very runway upon which the explosive power of God could land! That is one upside down Kingdom and then it gets worse - in its upside down-ness that is.

'I will boast' declares Paul. What? It means to 'live with your head up high.' Paul does not merely accept God's wishes with resignation. He lifts his head up and starts shouting about his struggles! Not in a pity party way, not in some warped penance (I deserve this) or proud 'Look how much this following Christ is costing me way.' No. He delights in all the things that show him he can't do it. He boasts about all the challenges that keep him dependent upon God. He realises

that Kingdom strength is only found in weakness and so he is happy to stay weak. This is part of the deeper magic.

I think Jesus put it pretty well in what we call the Sermon on the Mount in Matthew chapter 5:5: *'Blessed are the poor in spirit, for theirs is the kingdom of heaven.'*

Jesus said blessed people, those who possess the Kingdom, are those who know they are utterly destitute. They know they really have nothing, can do nothing, they have no power and have nothing to stand on or rely on. Blessed. This is the testimony of Scripture. Hebrews chapter 11 records this *'great cloud of witnesses'*, those who have gone before us and lived against all odds with the thing that pleases God, faith. It records that their weakness was turned to strength. They were chosen and used in their weakness.

It's very important to note here that we are not talking about sin! Paul was not delighting in gossip, pornography or anger so that the power of God would rest upon him. Any sin is not good news. Sin builds a wall to the grace of God and His power, it's not a doorway to its entrance. Thank you, Jesus, that through the cross God will extend grace and forgiveness to our sins - time after time - but that is not the weakness we are talking about here. Please underline that in your hearts.

When a person fails or makes a mess of something, someone will often remark (accompanied by a shrug of the shoulders) 'well, they are only human.' This is a downgrade of creation and a misunderstanding of the dependent relationship we were perfectly designed to fulfil. To be human is to be the very best vessel, the best temple within which God could abide. Humanity is glorious but never on its own.

The glory of being human is our utter compatibility with the most powerful being in the universe. You and I are wonderfully made, we have a wonderful weakness - that we can't do life on our own, that I am not enough for me - I am made for God, and Christ in me is the very foundation of this glory.

A few months after the death of Mother Teresa they discovered, at the Vatican, a huge number of letters she had written. They were an accountable and frank commentary on the life of one of the most revered individuals of the twentieth century. In her own hand she described a sacrificial life that was marked by years of depression, struggle and doubt. She spent her life literally washing the feet of the poorest of the poor in India, simply armed with a command to go and a trust in a God she rarely felt or heard from. She was weak, and her weakness was the perfect vessel through which to extend the message of God's love to the world.

We Christians contain the most incredible thing - we have Jesus in us, and our calling is to reveal Him to the world. We have Jesus in us not because we are so good, wonderful or gifted - we have Him in us because we have surrendered and have confessed our great need of Him. We do not reveal Him by being brilliant, stronger, more together or better than everyone else. It is actually the contrast between our frailty and His power, our being ordinary and Him being extraordinary, that shows Jesus to the world. Then people will see the gospel is good news, when they see Jesus and not us.

'But we have this treasure in jars of clay to show that this all-surpassing power is from God and not from us.' (2 Corinthians 4:7-9)

Years ago, in Victorian Britain, a Londoner hosted the visit of a friend of his from America. One Sunday morning they visited a church with a highly acclaimed preacher. As they left the visitor turned to his friend and said 'That man was amazing!' In the evening they went to hear Charles Spurgeon. As they left a few hours later the visitor turned to his friend and with tears running down his cheeks he exclaimed 'Isn't Jesus amazing!'

May you gladly embrace your own frailty, struggles and weakness. May you in this humble acceptance discover the treasure that is Christ, the Pearl of Great Price, the wonder of the world, and may He shine brilliantly through every area of brokenness, every crack and every imperfection.

May you show Jesus to our world.

Reflection on Weakness

By Kathryn

This last decade in so many ways has been hard for Matt. He often seems to face one physical barrier after another, none of which are easily solved.

So many times I have felt useless, unable to strengthen or support him through his physical sufferings. In the past some of these have led him to struggle also with depression. The frustrations, sleepless nights, pain and anguish were at times hard to live with. Sometimes I wished he would trust God more, other times I prayed a lot for his healing, other times I didn't pray enough. Sometimes it looked like trusting God for the both of us. Other times it looked like listening to God for how I should react or not.

I remember reading a book called "The power of a praying wife" by Stormie O'Martian early on in our marriage. Although I can't remember precisely what it said and didn't follow a formula for praying for Matt after I had read it, I knew that God had brought us together for love and for His glory. I knew that we were both committed to being married until death parted us, and so I knew that I needed to find more strength in God to be a better wife! I knew it was important in my secret place with God to bring him my heart and pray for Matt. Most of the time I find God directing me to 1 Corinthians chapter 13:4-8 where we have a beautiful description of love (read it in The Passion Translation, that is especially beautiful!). Mostly I would only get as far as 'Love is patient' and realise that any frustrations I had with what Matt was dealing with would melt away if I learned to be more full of the Holy Spirit and therefore have more of the fruit of patience!

Being myself generally one hundred percent healthy, having the 'super power' of falling asleep immediately and having a positive nature are things that meant I was not used to spending time thinking about or being aware of my own weaknesses. Over time God has helped me become more self-reflective and see that it is okay to know what I am not good at or need to improve on. We will have been married for 22 years this October (2020) and I have been so inspired, over the last eight years especially, to see how Matt has grown in grace, patience and love. He has learned to rely on Holy Spirit. He has learned to embrace his weaknesses. He has found a way through the dark nights of sleeplessness. Often having nothing to offer and yet finding that God's Spirit overflows through him despite everything else!

I don't know where we would be today if Matt had been fine? Our journey would not have been the same. My own weaknesses and your own weaknesses propel us into God's purposes. The more I know Jesus, the closer I get to walk with God, the more I'm aware of my failings and weaknesses. My humanity often appears so blatant and yet despite that His glory so prevalent!

Conclusion

*'Through followers of Jesus like yourselves gathered in churches,
this extraordinary plan of God is becoming known and talked about
even among the angels!'*

(Ephesians 3:10 The Message)

I saw it a of couple years ago. There were about 35 of us
gathered in our Community Centre to pray for our friend who
was dying of cancer. He'd had a rough life, made some bad
choices and struggled with addiction and broken
relationships. There had been a lot of darkness, but he had
found the light. Jesus had touched his heart and in his own
humorous style he was a follower of Christ. Sadly, as things
seemed to be finally coming together, that terrible disease hit.

At one point during our prayer time a businessman in our
church came over and knelt by him, laid his arm across his
shoulders and prayed words from a heart that was breaking
with the sorrow of this life, yet overflowing with the
unquenchable love of God. There was not a dry eye in the
house. On paper, these two men were so different. They had
completely different backgrounds and experiences. Neither
had walked in the other's shoes, yet they embraced and wept
as brothers; and I saw the Church.

There it is: the magnificent, wondrous plan of God. The thing we call Church and what scripture describes as the visible presence of Jesus in our World (the body of Christ). The plan was never stunning individual ministries. The plan was not even for great families and homes. The plan was always a people joined from every walk of life, throwing aside every conceivable barrier and joined as one family because of Jesus. Big family is the plan. A family that leaks glory, magnifies Jesus, and loves like God himself.

Our longing is to express this understanding of walking with Jesus, that which is contained in these imperfect words, to a larger family, to a wider community. To move beyond the trappings that religion places upon church to a daily lifestyle in which time, food, fun and Jesus are shared: to be the family of God.

The treasures, the deeper magic of this book, are written so that we can become *'a chosen people, a royal priesthood, a holy nation, God's special possession, that you may declare the praises of him who called you out of darkness into his wonderful light.'* (1 Peter 2:9)

The call is to be one Church. One family.

The future

The last eight years is the period during which most of the events of this book occurred. The context for the events, revelations and work, has been the little market town of Highworth and the church I serve – Highworth Community church

This is what the gospel has looked like for us and the desire is not to keep these things in our household but to share and nurture them in our community. This we have tried to do gently and graciously with our church which has become the runway where we have landed, the training ground where we have tested, and even the petri dish where we have experimented. Without them, their willingness, support, prayers, love and ridiculous levels of grace for me (I am a little weird), this book would have largely remained some good unrealised ideas.

A decade from now our children will all be in their twenties and maybe, if the economy picks up, they will have left home! Life will, in many ways, look very different and holidays for us should be a lot cheaper. But beneath the surface nothing will change. This 'deeper magic' will still be at work, influencing and affecting everything we do. Not one thing we have breathed and lived these last years will be set aside; it will just get richer and meatier (apologies if you are a veggie).

We have experienced how God loves to work in two directions at once: in and out, at the same time. He continually longs to break into the deeper recesses of our heart and shine the light of His countenance into the core of who we are. At the same time, He beckons us on: away from earthly comforts and manmade security into the adventure of taking His hand and meeting a broken world.

When we look ahead as a family, the thing we still want most is Him. Jesus. Recently we were watching the rather excellent Chosen TV series, a dramatisation on the life of Christ. As we witnessed afresh Jesus' ministry, so free and yet so challenging, we looked at each other and with tears in our eyes expressed our desire that He would just call us. Call us, just as He did the Apostles: that we would leave everything, lay it all down and just go wherever He went, giving all with no fear of disappointment or worry about tomorrow.

So, whether you are a teenager or retired, married or single, have children, want children, planning for children or not, you are called to this the deeper magic. You are called to live your life to build, bless, inspire, support, mould, serve, love and pray for church – the family of God.

I pray you reach the end of your race well. I pray you hold on and trust through all things. I pray you live not for the riches, pleasures, hopes or comforts of this life but for the coming King so that one day, alongside our family, we will all hear the only words that will make sense of this life… For one last time, read on.

And finally...

I imagine the scene.

Silence.

Then a sound breaks in, softly at first but quickly building, the immortal intro from Europe's 'The Final Countdown' begins; (if you don't know it quickly pop on YouTube - it will help).

Da-da da da, da-da da da da! Da-da da da, dat a dat dat dat dat da. Da Da!!!!

Powerful spotlights kick in illuminating pearlescent, rounded gates. They pick out a huge sea of eager expectant faces who are craning their necks to see who is next.

Suddenly a figure appears. They look a little battered and bruised but there is a fire in their eyes.

The crowd rises as one and the chant rings out:

'Faithful! Faithful! Faithful! Faithful!'

It's you. You have arrived. You have finished the race.

Ahead of you stands the one your soul loves. The one who went before you, stood beside you and for whom every difficulty and challenge was worth it.

Tears of joy blur your vision, as Jesus takes you finally and forever into His embrace and whispers in your ear:

'Well done my good and faith filled servant.'

Now it might not happen exactly as I have pictured it (although I am sure The Final Countdown will feature at some point) but we do know this. We shall see Him face to face and every fibre in our being, every hour, minute and second of our existence will ache and desire to hear those words - the only words that will validate our lives and how we lived them:

'Well done my good and faith filled servant.'

May you hear those words one day.

THE FORDS

Caleb, Summer, Kathryn, Ethan, Matt (left to right)

If you want to connect with us we would love that. We are open
to any opportunity to visit you and your group to encourage you
and reach out together.

Contact us:

www.wewillstay.co.uk

wewillstay@yahoo.com

Lightning Source UK Ltd.
Milton Keynes UK
UKHW020645040121
376125UK00005B/72